If The Cap Fits

By

Eric J Ward MSc CMIOSH

Eric J Ward

The right of Eric J Ward has been identified as the author of this work has been asserted by him in accordance with the Copyright Designs and Patent Act 1988

Copyright © Eric J Ward 2019
ISBN 9798603348223

Contents

About The Author P.4
About The Book P.6
Acknowledgement P.7
Introduction P.8

Chapter	**Page**
1 Legal & Moral Responsibility	12
2 Keeping It Simple	22
3 What Makes a Good Risk Assessment?	25
4 Safe Systems of Work	34
5 Management Systems	41
6 Health And Safety Policy	46
7 The Problem With Working Alone	49
8 When the Inspector Calls	53
9 Dealing With The Insurance Risk Surveyor	57
10 Effective Workplace Housekeeping	64
11 Accident Investigation	80
12 Loss Adjusters and Mitigation	89
13 Fire Safety - An Inspector Calls	93
14 Contractors/Subcontractors	98
15 Employee Involvement In Health & Safety	103
16 Ealth And Safety Gone Mad Mate	109
17 Communicating The Safety Message	115
18 In Conclusion	120

About The Author

Eric Ward was born in 1950; he attended a Secondary Modern School leaving at the age of 15. He drifted for a while from job to job – butcher, labourer, factory worker, ice cream salesman, window cleaner, dustman, van driver, the list is endless. Eventually he became involved in engineering.

Without any formal qualifications he secured a job with an American oil company as a hydraulics engineer. During this time he worked in many parts of the world including Egypt, Gulf of Suez, Italy, Greece, Africa, Holland, Belgium, Germany and The Gulf of Mexico to name just a few.

Later, when working for a UK engineering company, he became a key contributor to the building of the Stranraer roll-on-roll-off ferry in Scotland, being responsible for the installation of all the hydraulic systems and pipe work.

In 1989 he took on the position of manager within a German owned engineering company. As an addition he took on responsibilities for health and safety. This led him to take a post graduate course at Leicester University where he gained a Masters Degree (MSc) in Health and Safety Management.

In the year 2002 he became compliance director for a major construction and manufacturing company. During this time he was also a health and safety columnist for a European oil, gas and shipping magazine.

Following redundancy in 2012 he went freelance as a Casualty Risk Surveyor working for number of leading insurers. During this time he was also a

Senior Risk Management Consultant for the Fire Protection Association (FPA)

As a long-standing Chartered Member of the Institution of Occupational Safety and Health (CMIOSH) Eric has taught and lectured on health and safety management throughout the UK.

He now lives in retirement in a small seaside village on the North Norfolk Coast with his wife Brenda and labradoodle Bryan.

About The Book

This book is intended to help those out there who have been thrown the cap for health and safety and for those more experienced who just need to know there are others, somewhere, who are travelling the same stony road and have experienced or are experiencing the same challenges. This book is not intended to provide all the answers but, hopefully, it will point the reader in the right direction. This book cannot, nor does it seek to replace official publications. At best it can only give guidance gained through years of experience. This book is not big and bulky but small and practical. This book is not full of jargon, regulations and tongue twisting words but meaningful words and sentences for all to read, understand and hopefully enjoy. This book is designed to be read, put down and read again, folded up and put in your back pocket, brought out when there's nothing else to do and read over a cup of tea. This book is to be enjoyed, to bring a smile to the readers face and to give them some form of comfort in knowing they are not alone when wearing the health and safety cap.

Eric J Ward

Acknowledgement

In order to have letters after my name and to become a Chartered Member of the Institution of Safety and Health (IOSH) I have spent hundreds of hours studying, attending endless courses, reading reams of documents and books, listening to lectures all over the country and sitting countless exams. Now all this may seem very commendable, after all you don't get a Masters Degree and Chartered membership of IOSH without working hard and that's true. However, behind all the hard work and all the studying there was one person working just as hard, one person spending just as many countless hours alone and one person who was always there to hear my moans and groans, to put up with my frustration when things weren't going my way and to give me a kick up the backside when I wanted to give up. This person has spent hours reading my finished written reports, papers and coursework correcting my spelling mistakes and sometimes questioning the meaning of my words. In the very early days this person, on many occasions, would sit to the early hours of the morning, with Tipp-Ex by their side, typing my course work, ready to be submitted the following day. Without this person there would be no fancy letters after my name, no Chartered Membership to IOSH and no senior management jobs. So let me say to this person –

"Thank You" thank you for all the years of support all the hard work and all the encouragement you have given me, without you, my wife, friend and partner, there would be no book and no story to tell".

Introduction

I was perfectly happy being a one of the managers of a large German owned engineering company. I knew my job; the hours were regular and the money good. That is, until one lunch time when I was approach by the production director-

"Eric" he said "

"You're good at taking on new tasks"

Am I, I thought,

"How would you like to take on the job of health and safety officer?"

Before I could utter a word he then said-

"I'll give you an extra £500 a year"

Well money was a premium to me in those days with 4 children to keep. Without hesitation I said-

"Yes I would be glad to"

After all I thought, what's hard about health and safety?

Well that was over 30 years ago and I have learnt many times since that there is nothing easy about health and safety. In fact, health and safety could be described as one of the most complicated and unrewarding professions to be involved in. New laws thrown at you almost on a daily basis, publicised criticism from celebrities like Jeremy Clarkson and regular slagging off by popular tabloids. Oh, and I forgot, everyone you meet at work and play are health and safety experts, many of whom consider your job to be a doddle and a waste of time.

There are very few if any individuals who leave

school, college or university who want to be health and safety officer, managers or whatever title you may give the job. The majority are thrown a cap, amongst their other work duties, and told to wear it. They then find themselves wandering aimlessly down a lonely road with little knowledge of what to do, how to do it, or where or who to turn to for help. Their only reward being, most of the time, providing there are no serious accidents or visits from the HSE, they are left alone, sometimes for years, vegetating in an office at the back of a factory somewhere. If you feel I have painted a gloomy picture, then think on. During my 30 years as a health and safety officer, manager, director and insurance casualty risk surveyor, I have seen many a poor soul locked in their little world, a world where nobody takes notice of them, other managers consider them to be a necessary evil and senior directors see them as someone there to blame should things go wrong; they command little respect if any. So let me make it clear from the start, it takes a strong mind, guts and determination to become successful in health and safety management and it takes time, experience and hard work to command respect from others at work. There will be plenty of characters along the road who are ready to knock you down at the slightest opportunity and there will be plenty there to let them do just that. The name of the game is to stay on top, keep abreast of what's happening around you but, most importantly, get out on the shop floor and talk to people, the people at the sharp end. It's these people who will know if health and safety is really working in the workplace or if it is just being paid lip service and it is these people who can help you succeed in managing health and safety successfully. Get them on board and you are on the road to success but more importantly, on the road to helping people keep safe.

So why write a book, what's the point? Over the years I have read many books on health and safety, some good, some not so good and some a complete waste of time. However, the one thing most had in common was, too many pages full of unnecessary facts and figures designed to pack the book out and justify the extortionate price tag. I found them to have too many technical details, too many references to regulations, too many diagrams, and unnecessarily complicated. Few were fun to read, none made me laugh and few drew on real life experiences. Yes they gave me an idea of what was expected of me and they gave me things to quote, so I could at least sound like I knew what I was talking about but, the one thing they didn't give me was a sense of belonging, a sense of knowing there were others out there struggling, as I was at times, to get things done.

It is intended that my health and safety book will be a little different to the norm. You'll not find it packed with big words and mindless information, it doesn't have an extortionate price tag and it's not complicated or long winded. Yes there are some references to regulations and it does have some facts and figures, hopefully not enough to put the reader to sleep but, the one big difference you will find with this book, its compiled around true life experiences, problems and how they were dealt with and hopefully some funny true life stories just to make it that little bit more interesting and different from the rest. Yes you will find it a little unconventional and some may even find it controversial but, I can assure you it is truthful, factual and based on genuine experience gained over many years of working at the sharp end.

So with that said, sit back relax and enjoy the read.

Chapter 1
Legal & Moral Responsibility

Safety is a central part of management disciplines which has been a long time jostling for a place on the top of the table, or so we are led to believe. The 1974 Health and safety Act, which remains to this day our main controlling law, involved a laundry list of management responsibilities. Most of these responsibilities are still alien to many managers, particularly that rare breed of, hopefully declining, managers who feel that health and safety is something to be considered when production is at a low, you know, just before the Christmas break when the work load has slackened off. It's like they believe accidents can't happen when work operations are going at full pelt.

Many years ago I met a production manager who had 1 eye, walked with a limp and had a finger missing from his right hand. On meeting me he said-
"All this old health and safety lark is a load of old ####, all you need is common sense".

I later learnt that he had lost his eye whilst breaking up bricks with a hammer when not wearing safety eyewear, lost his finger in an unguarded machine and walked with a limp following a collision with a fork lift truck. Now common sense is a marvellous thing but, this guy was a living testament that it has its limits and he truly didn't know what those limits were.

It's been my experience that many of the managers and supervisors, I have met throughout the years, have had little idea as to what their true responsibilities were regarding health and safety. Yes they could all probably quote bits of Section 2 of the Health and Safety Act 1974-

> "Every employer to ensure so far as is
> reasonably practicable the health and
> safety at work of all employees"

Or words to that effect. But did they know what it meant? Probably not and why should they? That's was the health and safety managers job or so they thought.

Getting across to managers their legal responsibility for health and safety and convincing them it is part of their everyday responsibility and should be built in to the cost of all work operations, can be a lifetime's work, not many health and safety managers truly achieve this. Having said that, the one thing to remember is-

> "Keep trying but should you fail, don't let
> it spoil your weekend, life goes on, you
> will get another chance"

There will be times when it's a lot simpler to walk away and close the office door, after all your pay cheque will still arrive in the bank at the end of the month. However, that's the easy way and it won't say much for you and it doesn't take care of the employee on the ground floor who will, in time, should things be left as they are, have an accident because of poor management and because you couldn't be bothered to fight his or her corner, so the first thing to remember when you are given the health and safety cap-

"You not only have a legal responsibility but a moral responsibility also. If you haven't got the balls to exercise this, walk away, let someone else do the job.

It's a fact, if you allow certain individuals in the workplace to push you around and abuse your position, they will do so and others will follow. The only way to deal with managers who ignore their health and safety responsibilities or forever put them on the back burner, is to stand up to them. Try by all means to reason and explain but, if all else fails be prepared to fight, not physically of course but, verbally, with direct eye contact but most of all with passion. If you walk away you have not only failed your legal responsibilities but also your moral responsibilities to protect others who, unlike you, may not have a voice in the workplace.

Having established this, let's look at the legal and moral responsibilities in more detail, but not too much detail.

All employees are entitled to work in an environment where risks to their health and safety are properly controlled. Under health and safety law, the primary responsibility for this is down to employers.

Under health and safety law employers are responsible for health and safety management. The following provides a broad outline of how the law applies to employers-

1. It is an employer's duty to protect the health, safety and welfare of their employees and

other people who might be affected by their business. Employers must do whatever is reasonably practicable to achieve this. This means making sure those employees and others are protected from anything that may cause harm.

2   Employers have duties under health and safety law to assess risks in the workplace. Risk assessments should be carried out that address all risks that might cause harm in the workplace.

3   Employers must give employees information about the risks in their workplace and how they are protected, also instruct and train them on how to deal with the risks.

4   Employers must consult employees on health and safety issues. Consultation must be either direct or through a safety representative that is either elected by the workforce or appointed by a trade union.

These requirements have been in place since probably before most of you reading this book were born but, it could be argued that a great number of managers and supervisors to this day, have no idea of these requirements. This is particularly true when it comes to items 2, 3 and 4. If you find this hard to believe then think again.

I can record carrying out a casualty risk survey on behalf of a major insurance company. Their client was a very large engineering manufacturing company employing several hundred people. Now you would think that a survey of this type would be straightforward, after all they had, on paper, a rigorous health and safety system, a full time health and safety manager and full employee involvement, wrong! After just a short time at their premises I discovered that there were no risk assessments in place, not one. At the time of the survey The Management of Health and Safety at Work Regulations 1999 had been in place for about 15 years.

When questioned, the health and safety manager, who had been with the company for 5 years, explained that he had been working hard gathering all the information necessary but needed a new iPad to finish the job. I was astounded; I looked at him and thought-

"Five ####### years and that's your best excuse".

Not very professional of me thinking that way I know and I'm sure by the look on his face he read my thoughts.

Later in the day I attended the company board meeting to give them some feedback. When I explained they had no risk assessments in place the managing director nearly choked on his vol-au-vent, there was a complete silence in the boardroom-

"Why?"

Asked one of the directors,

"Your health and safety manager can probably best answer that" I replied,

Thinking to myself-

"When you get the answer your undoubtedly have the same thought as I did".

Yes I'm afraid it's true, that after all these years, lots of companies out there still don't have risk assessments in place and lots of companies have what they think are risk assessments in place but sadly are not.

Now having mentioned the employers responsibilities don't let's forget employees have important responsibilities too.

Most people know that employers have workplace responsibilities in regards to their employee's health and safety, far fewer understand that employees also have certain legal obligations they must meet also. Just like employers have a Duty of Care to their employees, those same employees have a Duty of Care to themselves and others. This Duty of Care is usually implied in work contracts and means that employees must exercise reasonable skill and care in (their) relationship with (their) employer and others. If an employee fails to meet their health and safety obligations, they can face steep fines and may lose their job. While employees don't have anywhere near as many legal responsibilities as their employers, they do need to understand that there are a number of obligations they must carry out. Essentially, these can be broken down into 4 types-

1. To work with the required skill and care, so as to not endanger others.

2. Use equipment and safety equipment for their intended purposes – do not misuse them in any way.

3. Attend all required health and safety training; do not obstruct an employer's ability to deliver essential health and safety training.

4. Report any dangerous working practices or situations immediately.

Now this may be common knowledge to someone who deals with health and safety on a daily basis but, ask the guys on the shop floor and he or she will probably only have a very basic idea as to what their responsibilities are.

I remember when I was a health and safety manager in the early 90's, purchasing, following risk assessments, a pneumatic hand tool for cutting angle iron, a pretty gruesome piece of equipment. The tool was used on a factory production line. The air lines etc were suspended from the ceiling to avoid tripping hazards and for safety reasons the tool was fitted with a two hand operation system. This meant that on each of the two handles there was a button which needed to be pressed simultaneously and held in position for the cutters to operate. Consequently the operator could only operate the tool when both hands were away from the cutter and safely on the handles. The operator, let's call him Tom, received all the necessary training and went about using the tool in production. So far so good you may think. A couple of weeks later I was walking across the shop floor when Tom called me over-

"Eric" He said,
"I have solved that problem
of having to use two hands"
"Problem" I replied
"Yes, I taped one of the buttons up
so I can do the job with one hand now"

You see Tom genuinely thought he was using his initiative; he had no idea his actions were violating health and safety rules and putting him and others at risk. Now at the time and being relatively new to health and safety management, I blamed Tom, thinking he was a complete plonker for doing such a stupid thing. However, time and experience has taught me that I was more to blame than Tom. I had failed to train and inform him correctly. You see when you have ignorance, inexperience and lack of understanding, you can have all the rules you like, they will have little if any influence on what really happens at the sharp end.

Throughout my career, particularly in my more

senior management years, I have come across lots of rules, requirements, systems and procedures. I have been presented with endless health and safety paperwork, mainly in an attempt to prove that a company's legal and moral responsibilities are being met. I have seen health and safety management systems that cover every imaginable event from the factory cat being run over by a fork lift truck to a train crashing through the shop window. Unfortunately I have also seen, on too many occasions, where these are stuck in a file in the office never seeing the light of day. They are in place to satisfy the authorities, insurers, customers and compliance surveyors, they bear no relevance to what really happens on the shop floor, in the office, on site or wherever the real work is being carried out. I have argued so many times that paperwork alone can't prevent accidents, paperwork alone can't keep employees safe. For accidents to be prevented and employees to be safe the information within the systems and procedures must be communicated to those at risk and appropriate training given, if not, why bother?

When putting any system or procedure in place or anything concerning health and safety, you need to ask yourself two important questions-

1. Who needs to know and
2. How can you get the message across?

Having established this it is equally important to establish a level of understanding. What you may

see as straight forward may be rocket science to another person. My advice, always try to aim at the lowest level. I always say-
> "Complicated is for the understanding of the few whereas simple is for the understanding of all".

In other words-
> "If the guy at the bottom end can understand then the guy at the top end should have no problems"

Chapter 2
Keeping It Simple

It's a fact that paperwork pays a big part in making sure health and safety works. Paperwork, systems and procedures lay out a level playing field in which to carry out our respective duties, or so we are led to believe. The truth is, you can have all the paperwork, systems and procedures in the world but, if the level of understanding or interpretation is different, than the level of implementation will also be different.

Many years ago when training a guy to operate a Fork Lift Truck I asked him to jump off. He stood up from his seat and did just that, jumped off!

"Why did you do that" I asked"

"Because you told me to" he replied

You see I wanted him to dismount in the correct way and I should have said just that but, I thought he would know what I meant when I said "jump off" Lesson learnt, never assume anything when dealing with people and their understanding of what you require of them.

Now when it comes to understanding, the one thing I have found difficult to understand on many occasions are risk assessments presented to me by some well meaning health and safety manager.

I can remember on one occasion being shown the risk assessments for a major concrete company. They were presented within a management system, ISO 18001 standards, or so they said. As I read through these risk assessments my head began to spin, I was going from one column to another and at the same time trying to read a scoring system that required an A level in math's. I ask the manager if the guys mixing the cement on the shop floor understood these risk assessment-

"Yes" he replied "Why shouldn't they?"
"Well I'm amazed they can, I have a degree in health and safety, teach health and safety and have carried out thousands of risk assessments and I don't have a clue what yours are about. If they are too complicated for me than I'm reasonably sure they are too complicated for your workforce" I replied

On another occasion I was reading through some risk assessment sent in by a tendering sub contractor. As I read through these assessments I came across the sentence "The timber structure is of brobdingnagian proportions" What the ##### does that mean? I thought. On looking up the word, brobdingnag is apparently a fictional land in Jonathan Swift's 1726 satirical novel Gulliver's Travels occupied by giants. The adjective "Brobdingnagian" has come to describe anything of colossal size. Now call me thick but, unless you have an avid interest of Gulliver's Travels how the hell would you know what this word meant? My point being, risk assessments finish up on the ground floor at the sharp end, its these people that need to read and understand the requirement, if they contain words such as "Brobdingnagian" then they are nothing less than worthless pieces of paper, in place to attempt to satisfy legal requirements and the ego of the originator.

The thing is with risk assessments; in general, they are so simple to perform that our brains can't accept that simplicity. It thinks, with all the regulations in place, which mainly revolve around risk assessments, that they need to look complicated to warrant the amount of work in producing them. On top of all this, there is so much conflicting information regarding risk assessment, its little wonder many become confused as to what makes a good risk assessment. So let's look at just that "what makes a good risk assessment?"

Chapter 3
What Makes a Good Risk Assessment?

A good risk assessment is a living breathing document which is subject to change based on new experience, new knowledge, other people's opinions and advice. A good risk assessment considers all significant hazards and aims to prioritise them based on how well each hazard is controlled. If the risk assessment judges the controls that are in place to be inadequate then further action will be required to improve those controls. The risk assessment is the place to note any further improvements that are needed for a task or process, gaps may be identified such as: a lack of training or insufficient lighting etc. The completed risk assessment, the one which is presented to the workforce, needs to be applicable to the task, easy to read and achievable. Take away any one of these factors and the assessment is doomed from the start. If it's not applicable it will be ignored by the workforce. If it's not easy to read it will be put to one side and if it's not achievable it will probably be placed on the back burner for another day, any day but not today.

Returning to the risk assessment sometime later to update it with further actions is a very good way of keeping a record to demonstrate the companies' continuous improvement strategy. Risk assessments shouldn't just sit on a dusty shelf where they are good for nobody.

One of the most important things when carrying out

a risk assessment is consulting employees and their representatives, where applicable, in the risk assessment process. They will have invaluable information about how the work is carried out; this will enable you to understand the actual risks in more depth.

So where do we start? Risk Assessing may seem like a daunting process and for someone that has never carried out a risk assessment before it can seem like a nightmare process. For example it's not uncommon to find people that refuse to put their signature to a risk assessment, fearing the unknown responsibility. I have had many conversations with clients about this and it's understandable when one considers the lack of training and information given regarding risk assessing.

The Health and Safety Executive (HSE) produce some excellent information on the subject of risk assessments one being 'Five Steps To Risk Assessing'. Within this publication the HSE state -
> "A risk assessment is not about creating huge amounts of paperwork, but rather about identifying sensible measures to control the risks in your workplace"

Never forget that first part-
> "A risk assessment is not about creating huge amounts of paperwork"

STEP 1: Identify the hazards

The first thing you need to do is identify all of the significant hazards associated with the activity or work task.

It's important at this stage to fully understand what a hazard is; so many times I have seen hazards confused with risks. Hazards are anything with the potential to cause harm, whereas a risk is the likelihood of that hazard to cause harm. As an example a knife is a hazard with the risk of cutting your hand, a ladder is a hazard with the risk of someone falling when being used or oil on the floor is a hazard with a risk of slipping. How likely the risk is, depends on the controls in place to reduce the risk. The knife has a purpose made handle and the operator wears gloves, the likelihood of cuts is low. The ladder is tied off and the employees are trained in ladder use, again the likelihood of a fall is minimal. The oil on the floor is adjacent to a busy canteen entrance door; the likelihood of a slip is high. I personally have always clarified this in my mind by thinking of the hazard as being the structure or physical thing such as a tool, machine, chair, carpet or a wall. In fact anything which you can see could in some way be considered a hazard. How can a chair be a hazard? You may ask. Well, if the chair is damaged i.e. a leg is broken then there is a risk or likelihood of falling off the chair.

This step is important and it is good practice to ask employees what they think the hazards are, as they may notice things that are not obvious to you and may have some good ideas on how to control the risks.

STEP 2: Decide who might be harmed
Then think about who might be harmed, for example: employees (or others who may be present)

and people such as contractors or visitors. Take members of the public into account if they could be harmed by your work activities.

Too often the poor old cleaner who comes in when everyone has gone home is forgotten. These people handle all sorts of hazardous substances and items and very often work unsupervised. Don't think that because your cleaners are subcontractors you are exonerated from responsibility, you're not! You are responsible for anyone visiting or working on your premises

STEP 3: Describe the Controls

Having identified the hazards, you then have to describe how the hazards will be controlled.

Generally, you need to do everything "Reasonably Practicable" to protect people from harm. Reasonably practicable meaning "Cost against risk". As an example and grossly over exaggerated. If an employee is carrying out a job and there is a very minimal risk of them cutting their finger resulting in a minor injury then supplying that employee with gloves at the cost of say £2 is reasonable. However, if the gloves cost £2000, supplying those gloves would be somewhat un- reasonable. You don't need to take actions that would be considered to be grossly disproportionate to the level of risk.

Choosing what controls to use are very often a decision that needs to be made collectively by management and employees but again, not forgetting, that controls should be reasonable and proportionate to the risk involved.

Many years ago, when first starting out in health and

safety management, I was asked if one of the employees could spray some items using aerosol paint cans. The job was a one-off and would only take a couple of hours. Now some may say "what's the problem it's something people do every day at home" Well work isn't home and there are certain rules which apply to the workplace, such as ensuring the health and safety of employees and others who may be affected by their work. I went on to the shop floor to carry out a somewhat minor risk assessment, just to see what controls needed to be put in place. It was straightforward enough or so I thought. The spraying was to take place in a well ventilated area, the cans were to be disposed of correctly and the operator was to be issued with an appropriate disposable face mask and shown how to use it, job done! Or was it? An hour later and wanting to stretch my legs, I went back to the area where the spraying was taking place. The guy was spraying away doing everything correctly, then he turned and faced me, I couldn't believe my eyes. He had cut a hole in the side of his face mask so he could have a cigarette without taking his face mask off.

Now there was a time when I enjoyed a cigarette but to smoke one through a mask designed to protect your breathing zone and with the risk of blowing your head off is just crazy but, the thing is with risk assessments, you can think you have covered all eventualities, but there will always be someone out there ready to pee in your tent.

STEP 4: Describe any further Controls / Actions Needed

Look at what you're already doing and the control measures you already have in place. Ask yourself-
"Can I get rid of the hazard altogether?
Or, can I do anything further to gain greater control over the risks so that harm is very unlikely?

Some practical steps you could take include: trying a less risky option; preventing access to the hazards; organising the work to reduce exposure to the hazard; issuing protective equipment, although this is a last resort. The list is endless, but again, remember to involve those who are at risk.

A company I once worked for had regular deliveries of Rockwool. This is a bulky material which comes in big rolls; it's used in industry for insulation and sound proofing. On arrival several employees were deployed to unload the lorry by hand. They would line up taking off one roll at a time over and over again until unloaded. The job was monotonous, involved repetitive heavy lifting and carrying bulky items on the shoulder, not a good idea. The job had been done this way for years without a question being asked as to why? The company spent thousands of pounds each year on this material and had a minimum of 2 deliveries per week. I contacted the supplier and asked if the material could be packed and strapped on pallets, at no extra cost to us, enabling it to be off loaded using a fork lift truck, "No problem" came the reply. One simple phone call and the risk of injury through manual handling had been reduced considerably, not to mention the labour cost saving. You may ask why no one had done this years ago, simple, no one had bothered, no one had bothered to look at what was being done and then asking the question-

"Can we do this better- can we improve?"

STEP 5: Regularly review your risk assessment

New equipment, substances or procedures can lead to new hazards. In order to keep activities safe it is necessary to review risk assessments on an ongoing basis, look at your risk assessment again and ask yourself-

"Have there been any significant changes?"

Are there improvements you still need to make? Have your employees spotted a problem? Have you learnt anything from accidents or near misses?

Make sure your risk assessment stays up to date. If you carry out a number of similar activities, you can produce a model risk assessment reflecting the common hazards and risks associated with these activities.

When the risk assessment is completed a signature from the person (s) carrying out the risk assessment will be required for several reasons. The signature is a demonstration of that person (s) commitment to that risk assessment accuracy. They are also confirming that they carried out that risk assessment.

From my experience it's very important that when

your risk assessments are issued and explained, to those with a need to know, that you also get a signature as received. It's far too easy, should there be an accident, for the injure party to claim they have never seen the risk assessment, a signature will prove they have. This is particularly important when defending an insurance claim for injury compensation or dealing with the HSE. Some employees can be reluctant to sign anything to do with health and safety in fear, should they have an accident, they will not be able to claim compensation. It's true to say that with good health and safety procedures in place, training and supervision, a signature can be used in mitigation should there be a claim and possibly reduce the amount of compensation if paid. However, a signature doesn't mean an employee can't claim for injuries received but, what if there's an accident and something was incorrect with the risk assessments? Will action be taken against the person that signed off the risk assessment? The long answer is: it depends on the circumstances surrounding the accident, but the short answer is generally: No! The Employer has overall accountability for activities in the workplace for which the responsibility for implementation is usually delegated to others, I say responsibility not accountability. If an employee carries out a risk assessment in good faith, and then works according to the findings of that risk assessment, generally there's nothing to worry about.

I have performed thousands of risk assessment and inspected even more. I know hundreds of people who have performed risk assessments; I don't know one who has found themselves in court for carrying out a risk assessment in good faith. Don't get me wrong, this may not be the case if you just throw something together without any due consideration of the hazards and risks involved, using it as just a paperwork exercise, do that and you could find yourself in big trouble.

If you were to ask your peers or if you go on the internet you will find hundreds of formats for a risk assessment. There is no set format providing you have covered all of the basics for the particular activity being assessed. These include, hazards, risks, those at risk, current control measures in place, further control measures required etc. The big thing to remember is, the finished product must be thorough, understandable to all with a need to know and conveyed to all with a need to know - not forgetting "Put into action".

Chapter 4
Safe Systems of Work

As the name suggests, a safe system of work (SSofW) is a defined set of procedures, resulting from a careful study of a task, namely a risk assessment. The SSofW informs how work must be carried out safely. SSofW are developed by taking into account the risk assessment(s) the people involved and affected, substances and equipment involved in undertaking a task, and then seeking to minimise or eliminate these risks further by providing a formal framework for employees to follow.

SSofW are typically laid out in a written document, for example, written operating procedures. They can also be more informal; verbal instructions, a list of do's and don'ts. However, for the sake of clarity, ease of reference, and demonstrating compliance, written systems of work are preferable.

SSofW ensure that all the steps necessary for safe working have been anticipated and hopefully implemented. They are designed to reduce human error. They prevent situations where employees attempt to cut corners, rush through a task or take unnecessary risks, reducing the likelihood of accidents occurring. So where do you start?

It would be unreasonable to expect all employees to maintain a permanent state of high alert, constantly examining their surroundings for sources of harm. It seems more reasonable that management systematically work their way through each area and process in the workplace, considering what harm may occur to their staff during the working day, commonly known as risk assessments. From here you can determine where SSofW need to be developed. All SSofW should be based on a thorough risk assessment, so it's important that all aspects of a particular task/job are examined and documented to make sure that no elements of a particular task are overlooked.

Make a note of:

- **What is used** (plant and equipment, substances, machinery, electrical sources)
- **Potential error sources** (possible human error, short cuts, equipment failure)
- **Where the task is carried out** (the working environment and its protection needs) and
- **How the task is carried out** (procedures, task frequency, training needs etc).

The compiling of the SSofW should be carried out by using information from the risk assessments, employee involvement, those who have detailed knowledge of the activity, and not forgetting product/manufacturer information etc.

The reason SSofW are created is to ensure employees do not suffer serious, possibly disabling injuries. Having a SSofW provides a consistent approach to each task as many safeguards are similar for certain risks, like wearing the same type of face mask for certain types of dust exposure or hearing protection in certain noise environments. These "repeat" features, in conjunction with proper training, assist in remembering the correct procedures. These are the first steps in devising a SSofW.

There is very often confusion and disagreement as to the difference between a SSofW and a Method Statement (MS). In my view a SSofW is a system that helps to prevent injury/illness, it is usually organisation specific and focuses on the work, organisation, equipment, management and the individual in the task/s etc. A MS is how the task will be performed by the individuals. As an example, a SSofW for fitting a door would give instruction on the personal protective equipment (PPE) to be worn, whether a 2 man lift is required or lifting equipment to be used and safety when using any particular tools etc. Whereas a MS is the way in which the door will be fitted i.e. held in place with G clamps while 6mm stainless steel screws are fitted to top and bottom hinges.

However, having said that, method statements have been adopted and are most often found in the construction sector. Here they were originally put in place for:
- higher-risk, complex or unusual work, eg steel and formwork erection, demolition or the use of hazardous substances
- providing information to employees about how the work should be done and the precautions to be taken
- providing the principal contractor with information to develop the health and safety plan for the construction phase of a project and have since replaced, in name, SSofW.

I think the argument of the basic difference between a safe system of work and a method statement is one that will continue for many years to come, look it up on the internet and see just how much disagreement there is. Personally I don't think it matters as long as the safety message is one of the same and is conveyed to all with a need to know

Personally I like SSofW; I would have SSofW in place for everything and very often did. It's here that you can really simplify the requirements of the risk assessment with bullet points, short statements and even pictures. A well laid out and easy to read SSofW is worth a thousand words falling on deaf ears. So what is a good SSofW?

It's a set of basic procedures that should be implemented before starting work and during working on a particular task. SSofW should be designed to protect the employee and others who may be affected by the work being carried out.

SSofW are nothing new we put many hundreds of SSofW into action every day of the week. If we cross the road we look both ways and only cross if safe to do so; this is a SSofW, if we take a young child, son/daughter etc, for a walk we will probably hold their hand in fear of the traffic; this is a SSofW and when we test the bath water before getting in to see if it's too hot; this is also a SSofW. These SSofW and many others come naturally; we don't have to think about them, we just do them. However, the work environment is a lot different, it's here we can come across situations that maybe we haven't experienced before, or tasks we only do occasionally. Some of these activities, if carried out incorrectly, will have serious consequences and may cause injuries to people and/or damage to property.

So what information should a SSofW contain? SSofW need to be detailed enough to cover most eventualities which could cause harm when carrying out a particular task, but simple enough to be understood and followed by all concerned. The purpose of a SSofW is to reduce risk, not to confuse the employee carrying out the task.

Will a SSofW prevent an accident? A SSofW will not necessarily prevent an accident but will reduce the risk of an accident. A SSofW is a reminder of what needs to be done before and during a work activity; a SSOW should be considered as a tool to carry out a task correctly and safely and in compliance with company rules, procedures and regulations.

Whilst on the subject of SSofW. I can remember once having the need to stop employees from wearing shorts at work due to the nature of that work, handling sheet metal etc. I carried out the necessary risk assessments and introduced a SSofW. The SSofW, amongst other things, stated that shorts must not be worn. The following day a manager came into my office and said-
> "Eric, go on the shop floor you may see something interesting"

I went out on the shop floor and to my amusement; two male employees were wearing, not shorts, but skirts! Yes it was funny and everyone had a good laugh but for me, it was also big learning curve.

"Make sure you cover all areas and get the wording correct". In my case rather than saying "shorts must not be worn" I should have said "legs must be fully covered".

What are an employee's responsibilities regarding SSofW? The relevant section on personal responsibility contained in the Health and Safety at Work Act basically says-
> "Individuals must work in a manner which does not put themselves or anyone else in danger. They must comply with all safety requirements advised by their employer and they must not misuse or abuse any item supplied for safety purposes.

This would include the use and implementation of SSofW

Devising a SSofW and providing appropriate training to ensure they are carried out correctly, will not only help to prevent accidents but will also help to defend prosecutions, should an accident occur, by providing evidence of the steps taken to ensure safe practices.

With fines increasing year by year, taking the time to proactively strengthen your safety system is crucial and developing effective SSofW is a key part of this. However, not all things go to plan.

I once compiled a complete set of SSofW for an engineering company. The SSofW ranged from manual handling through to working at heights. As part of my plan, to make sure these SSofW were conveyed to all employees, I asked the maintenance department to fix a large notice board to a wall adjacent to the canteen. The idea being, a folder containing all the SSofW would be hung from the board together with any other safety information.

Nothing complicated about that you may think. A couple of days later I received a phone call informing me of an accident. Apparently whilst fixing the notice board to the wall, one end slipped and fell. The maintenance engineer's tried to catch the board and in doing so broke his finger. You can't win them all.

Chapter 5
Management Systems

Most employers are aware that if they employ five or more people, a written health and safety policy is a legal requirement. Whilst the policy itself is usually a straightforward statement of the company's commitment to health and safety, the organisation and arrangements required to convert the intent into actions may be more involved. This is where a Health and Safety Management System can be useful.

The Health and Safety Executive (HSE) used to advocate a POPIMAR approach (policy, organisation, planning, and implementing, measuring, auditing and review), however the document that promoted this approach, Managing for Health and Safety (HSG 65), was radically revised in 2013 placing more emphasis on making the health and safety management system an integral part of how companies manage their daily business rather than treating it as an expensive bolt on measure.

The basis of this approach is: Plan, Do, Check, Act. This method of health and safety management is based on the theory that it is a continuous process, i.e. you do not simply stop managing because you have got to the end of the process. Each stage overlaps and feeds into the next as your company continually adjusts its processes to improve performance.

Stage 1: Plan
This stage is about setting the direction for effective health and safety management system, usually by

producing a policy that sets a clear direction for the business. It should help to ensure communication of health and safety duties and benefits throughout the organisation. Policies should be designed to meet legal requirements, prevent health and safety problems, and enable you to respond quickly where difficulties arise or new risks are introduced.

When compiling the policy think about where you are now and where you need to be. Set out the company's aims and objectives for health and safety, who will be responsible for what, how you will achieve your aims, and how you will measure your success. Decide how you will measure performance, consider fire and other emergencies and compile a clear plan of how you would deal in the event of such situations arising. Plan for changes and identify any specific legal requirements that apply to you. From this start point you should be able to identify an action plan of how to implement the policy.

Stage 2: Do

In essence this is about implementing the plan that you have put into place during the previous stage. In doing this you should aim to involve your employees and communicate and ensure that adequate resources are allocated to the plan, including competent advice where needed.

Stage 3: Check

Unless you check what is going on you will not know how effectively your health and safety plans are being implemented. Monitoring and reporting are important parts of health and safety arrangements. When monitoring performance do not just rely on reactive indicators such as accident reports. Whilst lessons can be learned from this, it is better to monitor proactively as well, as you may stop incidents happening in the first place.

Stage 4: Act
It is important that organisations review their health and safety performance as it tells you whether your system is effective in managing risk and protecting people.

A formal management system or framework can help you manage health and safety; it's your decision whether to use one or not. From my own personal experience, I have seen too many formal systems which have been just that "formal". There to satisfy standards, clients, HSE, insurers and any other interested parties. On many occasions I have seen these systems lying dormant until a couple of weeks before the next external audit, when the dust is blown off the folders and the paperwork brought up to date. I believe a H&S management system should be a working tool, used by all and more importantly understood by all, if not, its purpose is purely for show,, a process to satisfy outside bodies.

A good H&S management system must be functional and concise, with the emphasis on effectiveness rather than sheer volume of paperwork; unfortunately many formal systems are paperwork generated or made that way by lack of understanding. Having said that, whatever system you choose, the best systems are those which truly reflect the company, employees, the work process, attitudes and behaviour.

I once visited a large construction site, where the principal contractor was one of the largest in the country. The company had rigorous safety procedures in place and a formal H&S management system, described to me, by them, as "second to none". The purpose of my visit was to carry out a routine inspection to ensure my companies sub contractors on site were working safely and complying with the main contractor's safety requirement.

I was met by the site health and safety manager who signed me in and took me to the main site office. Here I was given a full induction, shown a safety video, given a safety test, issued with appropriate personal protective equipment (PPE) and given an induction badge to wear whilst on site. My first impression was very favourable, how could it not be? The site was clean and tidy, enviable induction procedures and all the resources necessary to make sure everything went as planned. Well my positive thoughts were very soon to be shattered.

I walked across the site in the direction of where our sub contractors were working. The site was in the process of constructing three large university buildings each six stories high. I inadvertently went to the wrong building. I climbed up to the outside of the fourth floor, where I thought our guys were working. As I walked along the scaffold I was suddenly faced with a dead-end drop. For some reason at the end of the walkway there was no safety rail, it was completely missing. I can say now I was physically shaken. If I hadn't have been

concentrating I would have fallen almost certainly to my death. I stepped back my immediate reaction, being to protect the area from others. I called the site health and safety manager and explained the seriousness of the situation. His reply-
> "I'm finishing off my pot noodles at the moment I'll have a look in half an hour or so"

I was fuming and made it clear that his lunch and his pot noodles could wait and he needed to get his backside into action now! I record my language was somewhat colourful at the time. Needless to say he contacted the scaffolders and it was sorted. Later I asked him what the site manager had to say about the situation. His reply
> "He said you shouldn't have been up there"

I was dumbfounded; they had everything in place all the procedures and systems anyone could wish for except understanding. In reality they had nothing; they were like performing seals doing the same thing over and over again without knowing why or what for. There's a lesson to be learned here -
> "Never judge a book by its cover or in this case H&S management system"

Chapter 6
Health And Safety Policy

You're trying to write your own health and safety policy and procedures. You know you have a legal responsibility under the Health and Safety at Work Act 1974 to provide a safe working environment. You know you need to have a written health and safety policy and procedures detailing how you will fulfil your obligation under specific areas of safety legislation. So, what's your problem?

The problem is what makes a proper and legal health and safety policy? I have seen health and safety policies the size of encyclopaedias, if you know what they are. I have also seen them the size of a fag paper, if you know what that is.

The encyclopaedia size ones are there to confuse and bore the reader to death and bring them into submission. They usually cover every unlikely event from nuclear explosions to earthquakes, I'm probably exaggerating now but, the point is, they are over written, over dramatised and over the top.

As for the fag paper type, well they are the finished product of someone who has no idea or doesn't care. I was once given a one page health and safety policy by a tendering subcontractor which purely said-

> "In pursuance of the Health and Safety Act 1974 the company will carry out all work safely. The managing director will audit health and safety regularly"

It was signed and dated - so they got that bit right.

So why do so many get it wrong? Put simply, some companies try to cover too much whereas others cover too little. Compiling a health and safety policy isn't rocket science; you don't need to employ the services of a so called expert-

> *"The policy does not need to be complicated or time-consuming"* (HSE Health and Safety Made Simple P.2)

In fact, if you have fewer than five employees you don't have to have a written health and safety policy.

A health and safety policy defines how a business will manage their tasks and workplace(s) in a safe manner, ensuring that any hazards are mitigated or controlled and individuals are unharmed. If you have 5 or more employees you need to have a written policy – by law.

Your health and safety policy should be comprised of the following sections

- **Statement of intent** – This is a document that outlines your company's aims and objectives for managing health and safety in the workplace. Your business' policy statement is an opportunity for the most senior director(s) to outline their commitment to health and safety.

There is nothing complicated about this, a simple one page signed and dated statement is usually plenty.

- **Roles and Responsibilities** –
  This section details the responsibilities for individual management roles including the

responsible person for safety, so they acknowledge their responsibilities for safety.

You don't need to get job specific on this one. You only want the responsibilities outlined as concerning safety. For Example: It is everyone's responsibility to work safely. It is the foreman's job to provide operatives with information concerning all hazards. This is the type of information that your health and safety policies should include, nothing complicated and no names, like John or Mrs. Smith are responsible for?. If you put names in the policy and they leave, you'll have to write it out all over again

- **Arrangements for Health and safety**
  Give details of the practical arrangements you have in place, showing how you will achieve your health and safety policy aims. This could include, for example, doing a risk assessment, training employees and using safety signs or equipment.

I can honestly say that in over 30 years in health and safety, having to deal with the HSE, loss adjusters, casualty risk surveyors, environmental agency local councils etc, I have never been asked by any of these authorities for a copy of the companies Health and Safety Policy. In my experience the Health and Safety Policy is usually only asked for by companies you are tendering for work or organisations such as Safe Contractor. That said I wouldn't want to be without one.

Chapter 7
The Problem With Working Alone

The majority of people with responsibility for health and safety, managers, officers, coordinators, call them what you will, work alone. Most don't have an assistant or deputy, most start off without any training or even advice. Consequently most will start to learn from the internet and various discussion boards coupled with the odd book, if they can get the expenditure approved by management.

The internet is without doubt a great producer of information and discussion boards are a great provider of opinions. The problem is, you don't know who is putting this information on the net or whose opinions you are listening to. You ask a question-

"How do I carry out a risk assessment for a guillotine?"

The answers come flooding back with various opinions which may be correct or incorrect.

Now if you worked in an office you will probably work alongside peers. If you came across a problem in your working day you would have your peers to consult with, peers you know and have interacted with over time. In other words you know their level of expertise or lack of it, but most importantly you can converse with them face to face.

The internet is a completely different animal. You ask a question and you get a reply, but whose replying? Is it someone of authority, someone with no knowledge or someone with little experience? It's a minefield and its little wonder that many new to health and safety and sometimes the more experienced who work alone, become confused.

Now you could join a local safety organisation, most are recognised by IOSH, and run some very good monthly agendas. The problem here is, if you're not careful, you could meet other confused people with yet even more opinions on the right and wrongs of managing health and safety. This is where you need a little logic, common sense (sometimes considered a dirty word in health and safety), life experience and some good training. Without this you will struggle and probably become one of the many so called health and safety professionals hiding behind reams of documents and paperwork.

I'm a strong believer that before anyone takes on the responsibility for health and safety they should have some years of experience at the sharp end. In my opinion, someone who has been a butcher a baker or a candlestick maker, in other words, been around the block a few times, will make a far better health and safety manager then a person who has been sat behind a desk for most of their working life doing the same repetitive job.

Qualifications are an asset and certificates and diplomas are useful for securing that job at an interview but, good old fashion experience and quality professional training are the backbone of a good health and safety manager.

I once visited a small engineering factory in Birmingham to carry out a casualty risk survey for an insurance company. I was met and shown around by the quality control manager who was also the newly appointed health and safety officer. During our initial meeting he showed me his NEBOSH certificate which he had recently obtained, he was obviously very proud of his achievement and rightly so too. Following our meeting I requested a tour of the shop floor. As we walked around he was eager to tell me of the improvements he had made regarding health and safety; new signage, safety policy pinned to the notice board etc. I walked towards an employee operating a pillar drill; to my dismay the operator was wearing thick leather work gloves. I ask the quality control manager why, he explained-

> "This machine is extremely dangerous with a sharp drill bit turning at high speed, if the operator touched the drill bit it would cut his fingers to pieces"

I replied-

> "If the operator touches that drill bit with those gloves on it will rip his fingers off"

You see, with his lack of experience he could only see this hazard with text book eyes-

> "There was a sharp instrument turning at speed which could cut the operator on contact – gloves must be worn!!"

In reality, any experienced engineer or safety person knows that in the majority of cases it's a "no no" to wear gloves while using a pillar drill as gloves can be an entanglement risk. Use gloves while handling the materials and securing them to the work table but, always remove them before using the drill. You see this guy was trying to do a good job; he had a qualification but lacked experience. To compound things, he had no one to turn to, or did he?

I have never been afraid to ask questions, I have never been under the impression I know everything, if I have an engineering problem I involve engineers, if I have a trailer loading problem I involve the lorry driver, the fork lift truck driver and any other person with some knowhow and knowledge of the task involved. This guy was working for an engineering company but failed to involve the engineers when trying to make safety improvements, big mistake.

You're only alone if you choose to be alone. Use the people around you, the people who have experience of the tasks, machines and procedures, use their knowledge, and listen to their opinions. Never be afraid to pick up the phone and talk to manufactures, suppliers or even the HSE. I have had many conversations with the HSE regarding safety problems, sometimes they had the answer and sometimes they didn't but, not once did they become all official and come knocking at my door.

If you do all this and more, you will never be alone and with a little luck and some time, you will eventually become experienced. But remember, you will never be experienced enough to say you know the lot and go it alone.

Chapter 8
When the Inspector Calls

The only way to protect your business from an HSE inspection is to make sure you comply with H&S law at all times

HSE inspections are on the increase. In 2017/2018, HSE inspectors fined businesses £72.6 million for breaking health & safety laws. They issued 3,883 prohibition notices. And they carried out 517 prosecutions, with 7% of offences resulting in immediate custodial sentences

However, even if an inspector visits, prosecution is the worst case scenario. But just in case you do get a knock at the door, here's what to expect when the HSE inspector calls.

The HSE will normally inspect businesses working in high-risk industries. These include factories, building sites, transport and roadwork's etc. So if you have not had a visit for a while, don't be surprised if the HSE wants to take a look around. This could be due to a previous incident, an issue raised by an employee, a report of a serious injury on your site or, in some cases, they are just passing and decide to pay you a visit.

For whatever reason the inspector will want to check that you are keeping your employees, your customers and members of the public safe. The inspector will ask about the health and safety issues affecting your business and what you're doing to reduce risk. They may, no, they will want to look around your site and inspect aspects of your work, too. If they are investigating an incident, the inspector will want you to describe what happened and what processes you had in place. They'll look at your accident investigation report and any CCTV or photographs that may have been taken. They'll also speak to your employees if necessary and/or read their witness statements.

Immediately after the visit, the inspector might offer you written or verbal advice on how to improve safety at work. Or they could issue you with a notification of contravention, which means you've broken a law. The inspector may then give you an improvement notice. This will give you at least 21 days to correct the issue. For more serious offences, an inspector may issue a prohibition notice. This forces you to stop any activities deemed dangerous, immediately. They can also seize items and equipment as evidence. Finally, the inspector can prosecute you. You may be taken to court and issued a fine or in a worst case scenario given a prison sentence.

If the inspector gives you a notice of contravention, you will have to pay HSE expenses for the investigation. This is called a fee for intervention (FFI). FFI is an hourly charge, at present, of £154. You must pay this within 30 days of receiving an invoice. You'll also have to pay FFI if the HSE gives you a notice of improvement or prohibition. The fines for prosecution depend on the offence you have committed. For example, in 2018 the average fine for breaking The Control of Major Accident Hazards Regulations 1999 was £846,250. Of course, the total impact on a business can be much greater. An improvement notice can force you to make high-cost changes in a short space of time. A prohibition notice can shut your business down or lead to disqualification of being a director for a set period of time. Even minor breaches have lasting damage. The HSE will register an enforcement notice against your business for 10 years. This can make it hard to get work with new clients and almost impossible to bid for public sector contracts.

Well that's the frightening bit over.

Speaking from experience of working in various sectors and various regions I have only had 5 visits from the HSE in over 30 years, 3 regarding accidents and 2 unannounced, now that works out at 1 every 6 years. I can honestly say, besides nerves, there was nothing frightening about the experience.

The HSE are not there to put the fear of god into people or prosecute for the fun of it. They are there to make sure the law regarding health and safety is adhered to. I have never met an awkward HSE inspector, I have always found them helpful and I have always found them reasonable. I have never had an inspector ask to see any documentation unless it was relevant to an accident or ask questions regarding insurance.

Having said that, I'm a great believer in playing the game. By that I mean, when an inspector calls and no matter how busy you are, start off with a smile and a warm welcome, nobody wants to be received by someone who obviously doesn't want them to be there. Always be respectful, they are doing an important job, don't be condescending, always answer questions truthfully and always start by offering them a cup of tea. It may seem silly but it's always worked for me and it costs nothing - other than the price of a tea bag.

Chapter 9
Dealing With The Insurance Risk Surveyor

An insurance risk surveyor determines the possible financial risks posed by offering insurance cover. At some point, your insurance company will arrange for an insurance risk surveyor to visit your premises and undertake a risk assessment survey. The resulting report will determine whether any improvements could be made to reduce the risk of future insurance claims. The insurance company will then communicate what needs to be done back to you through your broker, and monitor improvements through to completion.

Insurance risk surveys can be categorised into three areas:

1. **Liability** (or casualty) surveys mainly look at health & safety issues which might be affected by your business operation.
2. **Property** surveys concentrate on possible fire and security issues.
3. **Business** Interruption surveys look at how a disaster might affect your business, the way that you deal with it and how you might recover from it to trade successfully again.

In some cases, a survey might incorporate all three at once.

Insurance risk surveyors will undertake the survey, collate and assess the risk information on site, record assessments, collect photographic evidence and prepare a detailed report. During the survey, they can advise on any opportunities to reduce the risk of future insurance claims. They will also make recommendations to underwriters about any required improvements.

So what is the surveyor looking for?

There are 4 very common insurance risks that insurance surveyors look at:

1. **Fire and perils** – examining plans, construction and fire protection systems to assess the risks to a building and its contents.
2. **Accidents and Liability** – assessing the possible risks to employees, customers and visitors to a building or site.
3. **Engineering** – surveying mechanical and industrial plants, machinery and equipment for faults and risks.
4. **Burglary and theft** – inspecting business premises to check security and storage methods.

In order to prepare for the insurance risk surveyor, make sure you are available at the agreed time and make a room available for the surveyor to sit and ask their questions. A tea or coffee and some biscuits are likely to be well received as well.

An insurance risk surveyor will want to see all relevant paperwork. Prior to the visit collate all this documentation together and take a few minutes to re-familiarise yourself with it before the big day.

For a liability survey, this is likely to include your

health and safety policy, risk assessments, training records and accident statistics.

For a property survey you are likely to need alarm specifications and testing procedures and any security contracts details.

A business interruption survey will require a copy of your business continuity (disaster recovery) plan.

At some point the surveyor will want to have a walk around the premises, partly to familiarise themselves with the business and also to identify any areas which may require attention, they may take photographs while doing this.

It would be helpful if someone with the power to make things happen is present. In many cases, you may be able to deal with a requirement on the spot and avoid its inclusion in the survey report. It also demonstrates that you are taking the process seriously.

This is your opportunity to highlight the good points of your business, especially if they relate to the topic being discussed. It goes without saying that all of your answers should be based on fact.

The survey report is likely to provide you with a list of requirements and/or recommendations.

Requirements are must-do, often legal requirements, where non-compliance could result in a reduction or removal of cover by your insurer. You'll be given timescales to comply with these.

Recommendations are designed to comply with best practice but are not usually followed up.

If housekeeping and compliance standards are good, they may just do nothing.

Remember, insurance risk surveyors have probably seen it all before, so don't be afraid to ask questions, most will be more than happy to give you the benefit of their experience.

It's true to say that first impressions are very important. Surveyors will very often start their survey from the time they pull in to the car park. A tidy car park and tidy buildings will give an immediate good impression, whereas a disorganised car park and a grimy building will give an immediate bad impression. The building foyer can also set the scene. A nicely placed health and safety notice board in the foyer with lots of up to date health and safety information will be a big plus. Having applicable paperwork ready and available will also be a good sign to the surveyor as will good housekeeping throughout the premises.

I have always been a believer in first impressions, preparation and good housekeeping, have these in place and you will be half way there to a successful survey but, it doesn't always go to plan.

Some years ago whilst employed as a compliance director for a major construction and manufacturing company, the company I worked for bought a medium size timber frame company to add to their portfolio. The timber frame company had been poorly run and was in need of some big changes to bring it back into profit. In addition, the insurers had threatened to pull the insurance cover because of safety issues which had been highlighted in a previous survey report, they had one month to put things right. I was tasked with the job of getting things sorted ready for the next and final surveyors visit.

I travelled up north, where the company was based, to do my own in-house survey. On arrival I was dumfounded by the absolute appalling state of the whole place. I took pictures of everything bad and it was bad. I called a meeting of all managers. I introduced myself and then turned the lights off and proceeded to project my photos onto a screen. Picture after picture showed a state of complete failure to manage, rubbish piled high in corners, old mouldy sandwiches under work benches, aisles littered with off cuts of timber, half empty congealed milk bottles, tools thrown everywhere and waste bins overflowing, the list goes on. I finished my presentation, tuned on the lights and said-

"That's the factory that you manage,
anyone proud of it?"

There was a complete silence. I then said-

"Ok so let me tell you how we are going
to be proud of it"

I then laid down the ground rules, in no uncertain terms, and put a plan forward to get that place ready for the surveyor's inspection in less than 4 weeks.

Over the following 4 weeks, skip loads of rubbish were removed, walls were painted, floors painted, tools put away, aisles marked out and the whole yard made clean and tidy. Safety signs were put up, fire appliances and fire doors made visible and clear. At the end of the 4 weeks, although not perfect, I was reasonably happy with the result and ready for the surveyor's next visit.

The big day came. The surveyor arrived and with him a director of the company insurers, they meant business and were ready to remove the insurance cover.

I met them in the car park and took them to a porter cabin office. Here I introduced myself properly and explained that we had made some improvements and were continuing to do so. They went over their previous report and indicated that they were in no mind to be messed around any further. They then asked to visit the factory shop floor. We went across the yard, I opened the door to the factory and they walked in. The looks on their faces were an absolute treat. It was one of total disbelief. The surveyor looked at me and said-

> "I cannot believe this is the same place, I
> cannot believe what's been done"

Result, I thought. It was one of those rare moments when you knew everything was going your way. We had a tour of the factory and went back to the office for a closing meeting.

There was still a lot to be done but, by having a good clean and paint, many of the other deficiencies didn't seem so bad. I explained further improvements and timescales and they were more than satisfied. We sat back had a coffee and a non business chat and a few laughs. Job well done!

I escorted them to the car park and stood by their car shaking hands and saying a final farewell. As I did so, a delivery lorry pulled in. The driver jumped out of his cab, minus a high-vis, which was a requirement, and casually went to the back of his trailer, unzipped his trousers and peed up the wheel. My mouth dropped, I looked at the surveyor, and he

quietly smiled and said-
> You'll never win them all Eric"

He was right, you will never win them all but you must keep trying.

Chapter 10
Effective Workplace Housekeeping

To some people, the word "housekeeping" calls to mind cleaning floors and surfaces, removing dust, and organising clutter. However, in the workplace, it means much more. Housekeeping is crucial to a safe workplace. It can help prevent injuries and improve productivity and morale, as well as make a good first impression on visitors. It can also help an employer avoid potential fines for non-compliance.

Without wanting to sound too boring, poor housekeeping is responsible for the vast majority of slips trip and fall injuries, which cost the UK approaching 1 billion pounds per year. 37% of all reported workplace injuries were as a result of a slip, trip or fall, with 28% of all fatalities in the workplace being caused by a slip, trip or fall. On average approximately 50 people die each year from a slip, trip or fall and a great many more are injured, some critically.

The practice of good housekeeping extends from offices to industrial type workplaces, including factories, warehouses, manufacturing and construction sites. In my opinion, for health and safety to be effective, workplace safety should incorporate housekeeping, and every employee should play a part in that. In addition, it is vital that housekeeping should have management's commitment so employees realise its importance.

When considering housekeeping, I'm not just

talking about pushing a broom around the shop floor; housekeeping goes way beyond that and is by far one of the most important parts of a safety program. Good housekeeping can help prevent slips, trips, falls, fire, explosions and falling objects, the list is endless. Good housekeeping procedures can also assist when defending a workplace injury claim. So let's have a look at what we mean by good housekeeping.

Good housekeeping in the workplace is closely linked to a good safety record and how housekeeping is effectively managed, is an indicator of the safety culture within a company. Housekeeping not only makes the workplace a safer place to work in but, also provides a big boost to the image of a company. Effective housekeeping also improves efficiency and productivity; it helps in maintaining good control over the processes, and assists in maintaining the quality of the particular product. Having good housekeeping procedures is a win win situation.

There are several signs which reflect poor housekeeping in the workplace which can be easily identified. These include but are not limited to-

- Cluttered and poorly arranged work areas
- Untidy or dangerous storage of materials (such as materials stuffed in corners and overcrowded shelves etc.)
- Dusty and dirty floors and work surfaces
- Items lying on the floor which are in excess or

no longer required
- Blocked or cluttered aisles and exits
- Tools and equipment left in work areas instead of being returned to proper storage areas
- Broken containers and damaged materials
- Overflowing waste bins and containers, and
- Unattended spills and leaks
- Overcrowded desks
- Poor filing etc etc

Good housekeeping refers to processes which ensure facilities, equipment, work areas and access routes are kept in good condition. This condition is required for supporting safe and reliable work operation and maintenance. Additionally, during an emergency, such as a fire evacuation, good housekeeping ensures that the workplace escape routes are not restricted. It can also be said that housekeeping and cleanliness are interrelated. Reaching a good standard in one is difficult to achieve without reaching a good standard in the other.

Good housekeeping is an important activity in its own right; it's a visible indicator of the general standard of quality at the workplace, which can't be a bad thing. The standard of housekeeping is often the first impression which is observed by the visitors to the workplace, including, as previously discussed, the HSE or the insurance casualty risk surveyor. Poor standards in these areas also influence how the employees perceive the workplace and how they treat that workplace, if the company doesn't care why should the employee?

At the risk of repeating myself, let me reiterate the importance of this,

> "Good housekeeping is crucial to a safe workplace. It will most definitely help prevent injuries, improve productivity and employee morale, as well as make a good impression on the people visiting"

With this in mind, the importance of good housekeeping must be firmly planted in the consciousness of each employee, since a clean, neat, and orderly workplace not only contributes to the health and safety and morale of those employees but it also affects the overall success of the company, a good point to remember when pitching good housekeeping to higher management.

Without doubt, housekeeping has a direct link to efficient production and a good working environment. In fact, efficient production and a good working environment are complementary to each other. The elimination of inefficiencies and accident hazards caused by poor housekeeping in the workplace is necessary in getting the job done properly and safely. The attention to these important details, which are often overlooked in the workplace, not only contributes to a safe working environment but also has a big positive effect on the employees' productivity.

Good housekeeping involves every phase of workplace activities and should be applied throughout the entire process. These activities require the avoidance of congestion and clutter, such as, a tidy layout of the whole workplace, the marking of aisles, adequate storage arrangements, and suitable provision for cleaning and maintenance.

A clean and well laid out work environment sets the tone for work to be enjoyed by employees. It encourages tidy work habits; it helps reduce employee fatigue, which in turn is reflected not only in the quality and overall efficiency but, the reduction in accidents and near misses.

As previously said, good housekeeping will leave a good impression on visitors which will subsequently promote the image of the company. Customers and other stakeholders will have more confidence in the company since they notice that the work is being carried out efficiently in clean, pleasant, and well-organised surroundings.

It could be said that good housekeeping practices generally reflect the attitude of management towards health and safety practices. Good housekeeping reflects pride in the workplace, which signals that the company has a healthy and safe work culture. This is important since a healthy and safe work culture provides an environment at the workplace where the employees are not only at home with their work but, they enjoy the work and hence their work efficiency gets a boost.

The responsibility of housekeeping lies both with the management and the employees. Periodic and panic cleanups, such as prior to the Christmas shut down or lack of production work, are costly and ineffective and do not improve the work environment. Good housekeeping requires good and effective management of the workplace. Effective management is the reason for better performance, increased productivity and fewer accident and ill health. Good housekeeping will have a positive effect on accident statistics, employee attitude and accident claims. With good housekeeping practices in place, a workplace can be kept safe from potentially dangerous objects or substances, clutter and trip hazards etc.

Good housekeeping will normally results in-

1. A workplace which is cleaner, safer, well organised and has a pleasant environment

2. Improved use of floor space

3. Smoother and systematic workflow with substantial reduction in non-value added activities

4. Better inventory control of tools and materials

5. Reduced handling to ease the flow of materials and manual handling injuries

6. Reduction in wastages of materials

7. More efficient equipment clean-up and maintenance leading to lower break-downs

8. Safe environment for work and lower exposures of employees to hazardous substances such as dusts, and vapours etc

9. More hygienic workplace conditions which lead to improved health of the employees

10. Improved overall look and feel of the work environment, and improved morale of the employees.

Poor housekeeping on the contrary, creates workplace hazards which lead to various accidents such as slips, trips and falls, as mentioned previously, caught in-between objects, struck by falling objects, struck by moving objects, cut/stabbed by objects and struck against objects. The list is endless.

Furthermore, poor housekeeping also creates fire hazards which inevitably lead to increased fire risk and insurance premiums.

The starting point for good housekeeping in the workplace is the setting of the housekeeping practices and then training the employees in those practices. These practices should have clear objectives which are practical and attainable. The practices should comply with the regulatory norms and requirements. The practices should be safe and simple so that employees are motivated to follow them.

Good housekeeping practices should be planned and manage into workplace activities. As an example, the orderly storage and movement of materials from point of entry to exit. This would include a material flow plan which ensures minimal manual handling. The plan should also ensure that work areas are not used as storage areas. This avoids the employees moving the materials to and from work areas and thereby avoiding unnecessary manual handling. Part of the plan could include defined areas for different materials and frequency of material disposal from such areas. This can eliminate the need for repeated handling of the same material and promote more effective use of the employees' time. Often, ineffective or insufficient storage planning results in materials being handled and stored in hazardous ways resulting in unwanted accidents and lost time.

This may all seem difficult and complicated but it's not. In many cases it just takes some thought about what needs to be done, a pen and paper to outline the plan, some consultation with those at the sharp end, some time and a tin of paint to mark out storage areas etc. You may not get it right the first time but, you would have made a start and that's probably better than others had done previously.

Employees' training is an essential part of good housekeeping. Employees need to know how to work safely with the products they use. They also need to know how to protect other employees such as by posting signs, such as "wet – slippery floor" etc and reporting any unusual, unsafe conditions. If employees are not trained and involved then the whole thing is sure to fail.

Training needn't be time consuming. You could as an example train the team leader who in turn passes on that training to their team members.

There is a vast amount of free information available regarding good housekeeping which can be used in-house to train employees. There is no need to pay some high flying company thousands just to teach something which is freely available. If you look around the workplace, ask questions of employees and most importantly listen to employees, you may even find that you already have the necessary talent to train in-house.

The practices of good housekeeping must be maintained' and not be a one off thing. To be effective, these practices should be used on a regular and continual basis by the employees and management. One way to ensure that these practices are followed is to integrate them with the job responsibilities of the employees. As an example, each employee must regularly empty their own waste bin and not leave it to the cleaner, one named employee is responsible for ensuring a particular area is kept free of obstructions or one named employee is responsible for ensuring fire exits are kept clear at all times. An employee could have specific responsibilities for places which are 'out-of-the-way' or which are unmanned. Without special attention, these places are likely to be overlooked. The orderly layout of tools, equipment and supplies is also an important part of good housekeeping of which individual employees can be given responsibility.

Regular inspections of such areas and contact with those responsible will ensure that good housekeeping practices are being followed.

The major things normally included in workplace housekeeping practices can be described as-.

- **Dust and dirt removal** – Working in dusty and dirty conditions is unhygienic as well as unhealthy for the employees with possible respiratory complications. Also, if dust and dirt are allowed to accumulate on surfaces, there is a potential for a slip hazard. Regular sweeping/vacuuming of the workplace for the removal of dust and dirt is an essential housekeeping requirement. Compressed air should not to be used for removing dust or dirt off employees clothing or equipment. Compressed air can cause dirt and dust particles to be embedded under the skin or in the eye.

I can remember many years ago before my involvement with health and safety, seeing a man's hand blown up like a balloon where, for whatever reason, he held his hand tight over an air line nozzle.

- **Employee facilities** – Adequate employees' facilities such as drinking water, wash rooms, toilet blocks, and rest rooms etc. should be provided for the employees so that they can use them when there is a need. Cleanliness at the place of these facilities is an important part of good housekeeping.

I once visited a construction site where I was offered a cup of tea. The tea was served to me in an old and dirty used cardboard MacDonald's drink container. If that wasn't bad enough, when I sat down I notice in the corner of the room a decaying pork pie, next to the pie was what looked like a bottle of mouldy pee. I didn't ask to use the toilet whilst there.

- **Flooring** – Floors should be cleaned regularly and immediately if liquids or other materials are spilled. Poor floor conditions are a leading cause of accidents in the workplace. Entrances which cannot be cleaned continuously should have mats or some type of anti-slip flooring. It is also important to replace worn, ripped or damaged flooring that poses a trip hazard.

- **Lighting** – Adequate lighting reduces the potential for accidents. Dirty light fixtures should be cleaned regularly so that the light intensity levels are maintained.

- **Aisles and stairways** – Aisles and stairways should be kept clear and not be used for storage. Warning signs and mirrors can improve sight lines in blind corners, such as for fork-lift trucks, and help prevent accidents. It is also particularly important to maintain adequate lighting in stairways. Stairways should have hand rails, preferably round for adequate grip.

- **Spill control** – The best method to control spills is to prevent them from happening in the first place. Regular cleaning and preventive maintenance on machines and equipment is an essential practice. Also, the use of drip pans where spills might occur is a good preventative measure. When spills do occur, it is important to clean them up immediately. When cleaning a spill, the correct cleaning materials or absorbent materials should be used. It is also important to ensure that waste products are disposed of properly.

- **Waste disposal** – The regular collection of waste materials will contribute to good housekeeping. Allowing materials to build up on the floor not only creates unnecessary hazards but wastes time and energy since additional time is required for cleaning it up. Placing containers for waste near the place where it is produced encourages orderly waste disposal and makes collection easier.

Thinking of this reminds me. I once visited a company that used large cardboard boxes, obtained from the packing department, to collect waste from the production lines. It was an engineering production factory. I asked the factory cleaner how many he used in a day-

> "About twenty, I have asked for a metal tipping bin but no one listens to me" He replied.

When in the packing department I asked the packing manager how much a box cost-

> "Eight pound" he replied.

I did a quick calculation; they were spending £800 per week on cardboard boxes that equates to £41,600 per year. A metal tipping bin at the time, cost £1400 and would last for years, pay back 2 weeks. It was a no brainer to me but no one listened to the old cleaner, after all, what does a cleaner know? Lesson; always listen to opinions no matter what their position in the company, it can pay dividends and save your company a lot of work, time and money

- **Tools and equipment** – Tools should be cleaned and returned to their storage place after use. Tools found to be damaged or worn during cleaning should be taken out of service immediately to prevent accidents.

- **Maintenance** – One of the most important elements of good housekeeping and cleanliness practices is the maintenance of the equipment and the buildings. This means keeping buildings, equipment and machinery in safe and efficient working condition. When a workplace is neglected, such as broken windows, defective plumbing, broken floor surfaces and dirty walls etc. These conditions can cause accidents. It is important to have a reporting and replacement program to deal with this as quickly as possible.

- **Storage** – Proper storage of materials is essential in a good housekeeping practice. All storage areas need to be clearly marked. Flammable, combustible, toxic and other hazardous materials should be stored in approved containers in designated areas which are appropriate for the different hazards that they pose. The stored materials should not obstruct aisles, stairs, fire exits, fire equipment, emergency eyewash stations, emergency showers, or first aid stations etc. Also it is important that all containers be labelled properly. If materials are being stored correctly, then the incidents of strain injuries, chemical exposures and likely fires will be reduced significantly.

In my early years of health and safety I asked a factory labourer to move a pallet of materials away from obstructing a fire exit door. It was outside the factory, adjacent to the car park. 'No problem' he said.' Job done' I thought. Ten minutes later I was walking through the factory and noticed that the same pallet of materials was now in the factory obstructing the same fire exit door, but now from the other side. After thought- Proper communication is a wonderful thing!

- **Clutter control** – Cluttered workplaces typically occur because of poor housekeeping practices. Cluttered workplaces can lead to a number of issues which include manual handling, slip and trip injuries. It is important to develop practices where items like tools, chemicals, slings, and containers etc are returned to their appropriate storage location when not in use. Clutter is not only unattractive but, in a work area, it is also a serious threat to safety. Risks to the employees increases if the established exit routes and doors are blocked. For this reason, as well as to prevent slips and trips, waste materials need to be disposed of promptly in the appropriate waste containers and not left on the floor or propped up against walls. Aisles should be kept clear of all obstructions

- **Individual workspace** – Employee individual workspace, such as around a machine or desk area, need to be kept neat and clean, cleared of everything not needed for work. Many workplace injuries occur right in the employee's own workspace. This space is often overlooked when conducting general housekeeping inspections. Make a checklist which the employees can use to evaluate their own workspace.

Through good housekeeping practices, a company not only keeps the workplace neat and clean but also reduces any unnecessary risks. Good housekeeping will also save on a whole lot of resources which in turn helps improve profitability of the company.

It must be remembered that all employees of a company play an integral role in housekeeping. Therefore it's important to establish a housekeeping schedule. As a minimum, housekeeping should be required to be done at the end of each working day. At this time employees should be expected to inspect, clean and remove unused or discarded materials. In areas where significant debris build up is possible, it is important to establish a more frequent housekeeping schedule. It is important to train employees to keep their areas clean throughout the day in order to minimize hazards as well as reduce the amount of time needed at the end of the day to clean.

Like any other process, it is better if the standard operating procedures for housekeeping are formally written and well defined throughout the workplace. But remember, keep these procedures simple and don't bore the reader to death with complicated words and unnecessary detail. This makes it easier for the employees to follow.

Housekeeping should be an ongoing process, regular audits, walkthroughs and inspection schedules should be put in place to ensure this.

Good housekeeping practices can be difficult to maintain since production needs and busy time periods can mean housekeeping is put on the back burner. Additionally, a few individual employees who are not committed to housekeeping and cleanliness practices can make a significant difference. Hence, continuous, unrelenting management attention to these issues may be necessary to achieve and maintain the desired level of housekeeping within the company.

Without doubt a clean work area demonstrates the pride employees have in their job, the place where they work and the standard of safety at the workplace.

Chapter 11
Accident Investigation

"Every year people are killed or injured at work. Over 40 million working days are lost annually through work-related accidents and illnesses" (HSE 245 Investigating accidents and incidents: A workbook for employers, unions, safety representatives and safety professionals)

Accident investigation and analysis of work-related accidents and incidents form the foundation of a good safety culture. It is an essential part of the management of health and safety. Learning lessons from experience is vital in making the workplace safer and avoiding further pain, suffering and grief. If it is a serious life changing or a fatal accident the ripple effect is huge. It extends to the immediate family and friends, to fellow workers and beyond. Here I will try to offer some guidance on the key steps to take when carrying out an investigation of an incident or accident.

Golden rules to an accident investigation-
There is an old joke in the world of safety that says-
"The real reason for conducting an accident investigation is to establish who to blame"
Unfortunately, there are still some companies that still adopt a blame culture. This is very unhelpful in accident prevention. It creates a poor safety culture and under-reporting of accidents.

The golden rules when dealing with an accident are:
- Look after the victim
- Make safe the area
- Carry out the accident investigation
- Notify the enforcing authority if the accident falls under the Reporting of Injuries, Diseases and Dangerous Occurrences Regulations (RIDDOR) notification criteria.

Root causes of the accident-

The root causes in the number of accidents that I have personally investigated fall into two categories:

1. Failures in the Safety Management System

2. Failures by line managers in enforcing the rules

It is important to have an open mind; always base your decisions on fact, not emotion, rumours or assumptions.

After an accident, where an employee badly cut his finger, I asked the factory superintendent what he thought the root cause was, his answer-

"Don't worry about it, the guy is a complete ****"

I didn't put that down as the root cause in my report.

Resources to carry out an accident investigation-

Have a snatch bag ready for an accident investigation. What you require in that bag will depend on where you work i.e. construction site, office, warehouse, the industry you work in and

potential hazards present. Typically the items that could be included are:
- Site plans
- Torch (with spare batteries)
- Roll of hazard warning tape
- tape measure
- Travel first aid kit
- Camera to take photos
- Printed paper copies of witness statement forms
- Up to date phone list and organisational chart
- Pad and pen

Immediate response to take when an accident occurs-

When you are notified of any accident, follow these simple guidelines:

First and foremost-
- Make sure the injured person has all the medical assistance that they need

Gather the basic facts about-
- Details of the injured parties and injury
- Time and location
- Activities undertaken
- Workplace layout and materials
- Unusual working conditions
- Whether the risk was known or not
- Whether a Safe System of Work existed and was being followed
- Levels of competence

Actions to be taken-
- Inform the appropriate authority HSE/Environmental Health
- Find out who the witnesses are; separate them so they do not influence one another
- If necessary secure the accident site; block it off to prevent people moving anything etc.

Gathering facts-
There are three main techniques to gather the facts: observation, interview and documentation.

Observation-
Get to the scene of the accident as soon as you have been notified. Taking photographs is the best way to visually record the scene of the accident, take lots of pictures. When you are taking images of items relevant to the accident remember to show the scale and size; for example if it is a small object place an everyday item next to it such as a pen for a large object ask someone stand next to it etc. This helps to understand the scale of the items clearly. Label these relevant items. Make notes about the photographs as you take the pictures. Jot down simple prompt notes; these will help you and any other relevant people such as the enforcing authority when you get back to your office when compiling your report

Setting up the interviews-
Find and book suitable meeting room(s) to conduct accident investigation interviews. When you send out the invite to the interview, reassure the person that this is the normal procedure and ask them if they wish to bring colleague or Trade Union

representative. To prevent any disruption put up a 'do not disturb accident investigation meeting' notice.

Interview-
Treat everyone with respect and dignity. Explain the purpose of the investigation meeting and inform them that you will be taking notes to make sure that you have recorded everything that is said accurately. Put the person at ease: offer them a cup of tea. Try to be relaxed in your approach and if other departmental managers are assisting you, get them to introduce themselves and state their role and purpose in the meeting.

You may find it useful to have a flip chart in the room. You can draw a rough layout of the work area showing where the accident happened "x" marks the spot. This will make a simple and clear presentation of the facts and it will make it easier for the people being interviewed to give accurate information. When under pressure some people can get left and right, north and south easily confused.

During the interview use open questions, where the answer is not yes or no, to get an understanding of what happened. Open questions are used to get the person to open up to you, to explain what they know about the accident. For example:
- "Explain to me what you saw at the time of the accident"
- "What were the lighting levels in the warehouse at the time of the accident?"
- "What in your opinion could have prevented the accident?

This will help to focus just on the facts.

A number of people who witness the same accident will interpret it differently. Therefore, record the different points of view of what happened. Remember, you need to reflect on the facts and not the opinions from the interviews. Look at all the sources of evidence to see if they endorse what has been said.

I once carried out an accident investigation at a concrete manufacturing factory. An employee had fallen and broke his leg. At the time the employee was walking behind a cement mixing lorry. The lorry was used internally and never went on to public roads. The lorry driver came forward as a witness. During the interview he stated that he saw the injured employee fall to the ground after tripping on a piece of wood. I asked how he saw this when he was driving the lorry and the injured person was walking behind-

"In my wing mirror" he replied.

I looked out of office window and said-

"Is that you lorry parked out there"

"Yes" he said

"But you don't have any wing mirrors"

"Well, I didn't actually see what happened but that's what Terry told me in the canteen this morning"

You see this employee wasn't telling lies, he genuinely believed he had seen the accident. He had been talking to others and took on their opinions and what they witnessed as his opinions and what he had witnessed. When interviewing always question in detail and always go over the answers several times.

Documentation-
Typical documentation that you will look at during any investigation are: Risk assessments, safe systems of work, permits to work, method statements, training records, work procedures/job guides previous accidents in the work area, near miss reports , and previous audits. Depending on the type of accident, you will also examine things like check sheets, workplace inspections, and statutory test certificates and records, accident book, machinery check list, housekeeping check list and whatever other documentation could be of use.

Tools to understand why the accident happened-
When you're investigating a workplace accident, it's important to remove the immediate hazard, such as a faulty piece of machinery or an unstable shelf. But even more crucial is finding out the underlying cause of the problem. A root cause analysis (RCA) helps you determine the core issues that led to the accident. When you know the root cause(s), you can correct them to prevent similar incidents going forward.

A root cause analysis refers to the process of identifying the underlying cause of an issue or incident.

Whether you're investigating an employee who crushed their foot when they dropped a heavy box or one who tripped over a cord in a poorly-lit office, an RCA goes beyond simply removing the immediate cause of the accident. Performed near the end of an accident investigation, RCAs aim to determine the true cause of the problem, rather than just addressing the symptoms. A root cause is a fundamental cause that, had it not been present, the issue wouldn't have occurred. Identifying an accident's root cause and eliminating it should prevent the issue from reoccurring.

No matter what industry you're in, workplace accidents, especially repeat accidents, disrupt the workplace. An employee gets hurt and the work environment feels tense. You may even face fines or prosecution. Conducting a root cause analysis prevents similar accidents, and their consequences, from happening again. When you remove the root cause of a problem, your employees feel safer at work and you'll be protected from costly legal fees or costly damage.

There are lots of effective tools and techniques available to help you understand what the root cause of an accident was. It's a good idea to make yourself familiar with some of these for future reference.

Accident investigation techniques are essential. For example, if your investigation shows that the employee is solely responsible for the accident, it is very probable that you have not gone into sufficient detail in all the circumstances and different causes. I know from experience that in the majority of cases it would not be the employees fault. In the majority of cases the employee had been set up, not intentionally that is, to have the accident by poor communication, misplaced motivation or pressure by the management.

The process of investigating accidents will help you to learn from experience. By analysing the information, you can identify suitable risk control measures, prevent similar events recurring and share your learning. It will enable you to reduce the root causes of accidents and create a safer working environment where employees and companies can work effectively.

I once investigated an accident where an employee allegedly broke his leg falling from a loading bay. I have always enjoyed conducting accident investigations and I spent some time on this one. As I ploughed my way through the evidence and took statements I came across an invoice for loading bay repairs. Looking into this in more detail I notice that the loading bay shutter was not operational, permanently closed, on the day of the accident. How could this be I thought. If this was the case how could this employee have fallen from the bay? After a long investigation and taking numerous witness statements, it materialised that the employee in question, did in fact, break his leg playing football in the car park at lunch time and not, as claimed, falling from the loading bay.

Chapter 12
Loss Adjusters and Mitigation

"Mitigation is a reduction in the unpleasantness, seriousness, or painfulness of something"
(Collins Dictionary https://www.collinsdictionary.com/ dictionary/english/mitigation)

A loss adjuster is a claims specialist appointed and paid by an insurance company to investigate a complex or contentious claim on their behalf. They are responsible for establishing the cause of a loss and to determine whether it is covered by your insurance policy. A Loss Adjuster works on behalf of the insurance company although they do follow a code of conduct which demands that they should be impartial. They are not appointed to provide advice to the person making a claim – simply to look at the loss suffered and the context of that loss to the relevant insurance policy.

If there is a workplace accident claim against your company the loss adjuster will probably be in touch to arrange a meeting. At this point it is important for you to start to gather all the information you can in mitigating the claim. The loss adjuster will usually request documents such as risk assessments, safe systems of work, machinery check lists, safety audit reports, a copy of the accident book report, RIDDOR report, maintenance records, in fact anything relevant to the accident. A good loss adjuster will go through the documentation with a fine-toothed comb, reading everything to see if anything is missing, if anything suggests that the claimant has had prior injuries or that the claimant is malingering. A loss adjuster will not make a settlement offer and will not respond to a settlement demand without everything that's necessary to validate the workplace injury case. At the same time he will be looking to see the company have everything in place and that all necessary training, information and supervision were given to the claimant. Here the loss adjuster is looking to contribute blame or some blame on the claimant known as "Contributory Negligence".

Contributory negligence is where the claimant (employee) can prove that the defendant (company) was negligent, but the defendant can prove that the claimant is partially to blame. As such the liability for compensation will be reduced accordingly.

As an example, Bill, when working, fails to wear the safety equipment he has been issued and trained to wear. An accident occurs for other reasons, but the failure to wear safety equipment contributed to the injury, not the accident. If Bills claim is upheld by the court, the defendant could suggest that any damages awarded to Bill should be reduced by an amount that represents the portion of the blame assumed. If Bill is found to have contributed by 20 per cent, that same 20 per cent will be deducted from the compensation he receives. So, instead of receiving for instance, £2000, he will receive £1600.

Earlier we discussed good housekeeping; I would argue that having all the relevant documentation at hand, having copies readily available and in order, ready for the loss adjuster, is, in itself, good housekeeping. It sets a good impression, saves time and leaves the loss adjuster in a good frame of mind, not a bad thing when you are fighting a claim. However, sometimes you can do all that is possible and still lose the battle.

I received a claim from an employee who claimed he fell and hurt his knee whilst carrying an object, I set about my investigation.

The claimant had been trained in manual handling, there was even a video of him in the training session, he had been trained in good housekeeping, he was personally responsible for completing a daily housekeeping check list before each shift, he had signed all appropriate documentation, there were no witnesses to his accident and he retrospectively completed the accident book. No claim to be answered I thought, wrong! No matter how hard I argued with the loss adjuster he felt that for the amount of compensation which would be offered, about £1500, it wasn't worth defending. I was completely shattered by this. Here we were with a blatant false claim and our insurers were not willing to fight our corner. They argued that it wasn't worth the trouble. I argued it would give others the same idea and in turn create a claims culture, which we didn't have at present, and then they would have a problem.

I can remember another time when an employee claimed he was hit by a fork lift truck. He was taken to hospital by ambulance and released later that day.

When carrying out my investigation one witness said-
> "As Tom walked past the fork lift truck he strategically placed himself on the floor and started to cry out loud"

A couple of weeks later the injured employee came into work to make a statement. He was supported by 2 walking sticks and could only walk very slowly. He claimed the fork lift truck drove past at speed and hit him in the side causing a back injury. I was somewhat suspicious of his claim and employed a private detective. A few days later the private detective came back to me with some video footage. It showed the so called injured employee loading their car with golf clubs, driving off to the golf course and playing a round of golf. Got you I thought, wrong again! When I showed this to the loss adjuster he was of the opinion that it was a breach of privacy and the court wouldn't look kindly at videoing someone without their permission. Madness, here we had a blatant fraudulent claim, call it what you like, and we couldn't do anything about it.

I have many examples of this type of thing and at times it made me want to chuck the towel in but, you always need to remember, you're not just there to defend claims but to protect people to, the vast majority of people who are honest, hard working and deserve a safe working environment. The others will be caught in the net eventually.

Chapter 13
Fire Safety - An Inspector Calls

Local Fire and Rescue Services conduct regular fire safety inspections on business premises to ensure that they comply with The Regulatory Reform (Fire Safety) Order 2005. This will involve a visit from a representative of the Fire and Rescue Service who will carry out an inspection of the building. If you've never had one before, here's what you can expect from a fire safety inspection, should an inspector come calling.

So what's the role of the Fire Safety Inspector? Titles tend to differ depending on which Fire & Rescue Service they belong to but you'll often hear them described as fire safety inspectors or fire safety enforcement officers. They are usually experienced fire fighters with an additional understanding of building construction and their role is to enforce fire safety law.

A fire safety inspector has the right to enter any workplace at any reasonable hour, without giving notice. Although in the majority of cases they will call to make arrangements.

A fire safety inspector will check out the workplace, the activities undertaken there and your management of fire safety. They'll also audit your fire risk assessment to ensure that you're complying with fire safety law. It's likely that they will assess the structure and construction of the building, review escape routes, examine the means of raising the alarm in the event of fire and talk to your employees about their roles and the actions they will need to take in the event of a fire.

If a breach of fire safety legislation is found, a fire safety inspector can take action in several ways. They might deal with minor matters informally, offering help and advice. For more serious non-compliance, they can issue formal notices or take measures to enforce the law there and then. Notices for serious breaches can restrict or prohibit use of the workplace until such time as the improvements or changes required have been carried out, or, in the worst cases, initiate prosecution if you have failed to comply with fire safety legislation.

Given that it could happen at any time, it's important to make sure that you can access the relevant paperwork and have the answers to the questions they're likely to ask.

Some important things to remember are:
- Someone in your company must be the 'Responsible Person'. For most companies, this will be the employer or any other person who may have control of fire safety.
- Ensure the Responsible Person is competent and has carried out a Fire Risk Assessment (FRA) of your business premises.
- Review the FRA regularly – once a year is about right unless circumstances change.

As the name suggests, a fire risk assessment is an assessment of the risks from fire and involves a process that takes reasonable steps to remove or reduce any risks.

There are 5 useful steps that you can follow when putting together an FRA:
1. Identify the fire hazards
2. Identify people at risk
3. Evaluate, remove or reduce the risks
4. Record your findings and prepare an emergency plan with training
5. Review and update the fire risk assessment regularly

There is no legally prescribed format for the FRA but some Fire Services do have work examples, it's worth asking your local fire service.

When dealing with the fire inspector it's important to remember that they are there to help. While any problems that they might find are likely to cost money to put right, it's all in the best interests of you and your employees. With this in mind, here are a few tips for when an inspector calls:

- **BE FRIENDLY**
  Make them a cup of tea and don't be defensive or obstructive. If there's one thing I know about fire inspectors, they love a cup of tea.
- **BE ORGANISED**
  Think back about what was said previously about housekeeping, have your documents in one place, including the fire risk assessment, general workplace risk assessments and statutory test certificates for fire alarms, emergency lighting and sprinkler systems etc.

- **BE PROACTIVE**
  Ask the fire safety inspector for advice or help. I know from experience they love people who are keen to learn. While they are there to enforce the law, part of their role is also to offer guidance for businesses to comply with fire safety.
- **BE CALM**
  If a breach of fire safety law is found, ask the fire officer to help you comply with any minor issues. They can also provide you with any advice in writing after the inspection.
- **SHOW OFF**
  If you have made any improvements to fire safety, no matter how small, let the fire officer know.
- **BE HONEST**
  Don't try to hide things, be truthful, these people know their job and will catch you out if need be.

I have had many fire inspections and I have always prepared things in the same way and it has never failed me once-

- Take copies all necessary paperwork and placed them in a file ready to hand to the inspector. Make sure test records are up to date
- **WALK THE WHOLE WORK AREA –**
- All fire signs are in place and visible
- All fire exits are clear and unlocked
- All fire extinguishers are clear and visible
- All fire doors are working. Open the door, let go, it should close within 10 seconds
- All fire door seals are in good order.

- Stairways are clear of obstacles
- Under stairs are clear of accumulated rubbish
- Escape routes are clear

If you do that much before an inspection you are half way there. Preparation isn't rocket science, it just takes a little time and some thought. But it doesn't always go to plan.

I remember once spending a couple of days getting ready for a fire inspection. The day came and I was well prepared. On arrival of the inspector, we had a chat and a cup of tea in the canteen. Following this we made our way to the factory floor to carry out the inspection. During the inspection he commented on how tidy the factory was and said-

> "I don't think I'm going to find a problem here".

I've cracked it I thought.

We completed the factory inspection and he, and myself, were very pleased, no problems. Now for the offices, shouldn't be a problem there I thought. How wrong can you be?

We stood in the main office and he was looking at the fire appliance location map-

> "Shouldn't there be a dry powder extinguisher on that wall?" He said
>
> "Yes there should be and there is" I replied. "But unfortunately someone is using it as a coat hook"

All the planning, all that work to get things right, just for one individual to spoil the day by hanging their coat on the fire extinguisher.   It was a minor thing but an annoying thing. After that I never forgot to double check the offices.

Chapter 14
Contractors/Subcontractors

There is an important distinction between using contractors and subcontractors. Contractors provide agreed services to a client for a set fee and usually for a set duration under a contract for services. Many businesses typically use contractors for:

- building work
- catering
- cleaning
- gardening
- marketing services
- IT maintenance and support
- security services
- recruitment

Subcontractors undertake a contract from the contractor. Subcontractors undertake work that a contractor cannot do but for which the contractor is responsible. Subcontractors can be anything from an individual self-employed person eg a plumber carrying out work for a building contractor to a national company. A subcontractor has a contract with the contractor for the services provided. For example, a building contractor may hire a subcontractor to complete the electrical wiring part of the contractors building job. The contractor is responsible to the client for the building job, including the part performed by the subcontractor.

In any relationship between a company and a

contractor, both parties will have duties under health and safety law. If the contractor uses subcontractors to carry out some or all of the work, all parties, company, contractor and subcontractor, will have some health and safety responsibilities. To ensure contractors or subcontractors health and safety you must-

- Identify the requirements of the job and assess the risks
- Decide what information and training is required
- As the Company (client), select an appropriate contractor and ascertain their health and safety policies and procedures
- As the contractor, find out about subcontractors' competence
- Review the way work is carried out and the risk assessments

To ensure that there is co-operation and co-ordination at all times between you, your staff, contractors, subcontractors, you should-

- Provide all parties with information, instruction and training on anything that may affect health and safety
- Make the contractors/subcontractors aware of your health and safety procedures and policies
- Provide management and supervision to ensure the safety of contractors/subcontractors

The HSE have some good guidance on the subject of working with contractors.

I can't stress enough the importance of ensuring contractors/subcontractors are competent, fully insured, in compliance with all health and safety regulations and trustworthy. You can have the best health and safety system and accident statistics in the world but, an incompetent contractor/subcontractor can put pay to that in seconds. I have dealt with contractor/subcontractors for many years and in my experience they will never have the devotion, interest or concern for health and safety as you do as the company (client). Yes some are good, some very competent and some are very professional but, there are a lot who have no concerns at all for your health and safety procedures, these are the ones you don't want to employ. So vetting is very important.

Vetting needn't be complicated; after all you are just looking for competence and compliance. But there are some basic questions you need to ask-

1. Do they have up to date liability insurance?
2. If employing 5 or more, do they have a signed and dated health and safety policy?
3. Do they have up to date risk assessments?
4. Do they have an organisation structure, directors, managers, supervisors, foremen etc?
5. Who has responsibility for health and safety?
6. Who is the individual or organisation that acts as the Competent Person?

7. What health and safety training has been given to employees over the last 2 years?
8. Have they had any RIDDOR incidents in the last 3 years?
9. Have they had any involvement with the HSE in the last 3 years?
10. Do they have written health and safety procedures for working on clients sites?

All of this and more can be included on a questionnaire. Remember to ask for copies of relevant documentation.

As well as a questionnaire it is equally important to have some form of site health and safety rules/conditions to issue to contractors / subcontractors. These rules should list the do's and don'ts of health and safety whilst on your site. As an example it could include information on-

- Induction
- General Requirements
- Entry on to site
- Housekeeping
- Fire Precautions
- Electrical Work
- Operating Processes
- Accident Reporting
- Near Misses
- Waste Disposal
- Alcohol & Drugs
- Working from Height
- Scaffolding

- Fall Arrest Systems
- Ladders
- Lifting Equipment
- Personal Protective Equipment
- Noise
- COSHH
- HSE Inspections

Issuing this information and obtaining a signature prevents the old excuse "I didn't know"

Chapter 15
Employee Involvement In Health & Safety

You will often hear talk about the benefits of encouraging a positive health and safety culture in the workplace by involving employees. It might seem obvious, but consulting your employees on workplace health and safety is often overlooked or forgotten. Strong communication and employee involvement can bring about important positive changes to the health and safety culture of a business.

Communication between employers and employees about matters of health and safety are important factors. Areas that need improving can be identified, and successes can be monitored more efficiently if everyone is involved. If employees are involved in the company's health and safety concerns, they can better understand why safety policies are in place. By being involved employers can help identify hazards before they cause accidents. By encouraging active employee involvement, both parties can be encouraged to raise health and safety concerns. By making decisions and discussing issues together, both parties can better understand the health and safety procedures, and why precautions are in place.

It's easy to feel a bit dubious about encouraging employees to get involved in health and safety decisions, after all, we all know there are some employees whose only aim in life is to make your life a misery. However, you need to go beyond them and reach out to the majority of employees who can contribute considerably. Get them on board and the pain in the backside ones will have to follow.

It's not always easy to involve and get employees involved; it's a process that needs a lot of thought. The one thing you don't want is lots of people involved who are problem finders, yes if there is a problem you need to know but, it's also good to have some problem solvers.

Many years ago I went to work for a company as a group Health, Safety and Security Manager. The company had a very strong and somewhat militant union. Accident claims were beyond belief; they even held a monthly surgery in a local pub for employees to register claims. It was my remit to reduce these claims.

On the first day of starting with the company I was confronted in my office by the senior shop steward who gave me a list of demands. He told me the company was rubbish, they had no thought about health and safety and they didn't listen to him or care and what was needed was union involvement because the union knew how to put things right. Strangely, despite all of his complaints, he had been with the company for over 25 years.

At the next board meeting I requested that I could seconder the senior shop steward into my department as and when required. After some discussion my request was granted.

Now I had an assistant manager, H&S coordinator, a secretary and an occupational nurse working for me at the time, they were horrified at the thought of this rather loud person coming into our department as and when, obviously they feared the worst.

I quickly arranged a meeting with the senior shop steward before he got to hear of my intentions and we sat and talked. During the meeting I allowed him to do most of the talking. He told me of the problems, especially regarding manual handling and what should and shouldn't be done about it. He told me that while nothing was done accident claims would rise again and again. I think at this point he thought I was a complete push over and a little timid.

I looked at him and said-
> "If you had the chance could you sort the manual handling problem out and reduce accident claims"

He replied-
> "No problem I have been telling them for years what's wrong and how to deal with it"

There was a silence, I looked him in straight in the eye and said-
> "Would you like that chance, the chance to sort the manual handling out?"

He laughed-
> "Fat chance of that happening"
>
> "OK, I agree with everything you said"

His face suddenly had a puzzled look, if to say-
> "Did I hear right"

I leant across the table, again looking him straight in the eye, and said-

"As of now you're working for me for the next 3 months at least and I want you to go out there and get that manual handling sorted just like you have always wanted to do"

At this point "If but if but" comes to mind.

"I need to get my supervisors permission" he said

"No need it's all sorted, just go out there and do it" I replied.

He got up and started to walk towards the door, I called to him-

"When you've completed the manual handling risk assessments and the root cause analysis for any related accident I will have a look before signing them off"

He went out the door closing it quietly. 2 Minutes later, the door slowly opened, his head popped in and he said-

"How do I do that then?"

I replied- "Not so easy is it"

We sat down, this time he listened, and we decided that the best way to go about things was as a team helping each other with health and safety our priority.

Together and with the setting up of employee health and safety committees we, as a team, reduced accidents in the workplace by 99% in just 12 months. As for industrial accident claims, they vanished.

With employee involvement the benefits can be far reaching, both for the employer and the employee:

- **Lower accident rates**
  The HSE have found that accident rates are lower in companies where employees feel like they have a say in health and safety matters compared to workplaces with no employee involvement.
- **More positive health and safety climate**
  In workplaces with employee involvement, the HSE found that employees felt encouraged to raise H&S concerns.
- **Better control of risks**
  Control of slips, trips and falls was found to be effective in 76% of workplaces where employees felt they were involved in decisions, compared to 40% if they felt they were rarely or never consulted.
- **Greater awareness of risks**
  By involving employees in health and safety discussions, employees are more aware of the risks in the workplace and can take better care around hazards.
- **Improved morale**
  By involving employees in workplace health and safety decisions, employers can demonstrate that they do care about their employees' welfare and well-being, which can lead to improved workplace morale. Improved morale brings about its own benefits, such as improved productivity and lower staff turnover rates.

Employers have a lot to gain by encouraging employee involvement in health and safety decisions in the workplace. Encouraging a positive health and safety culture can bring about several **benefits** and companies stand to gain a lot from employee engagement with issues of health and safety.

Chapter 16
Ealth And Safety Gone Mad Mate

We have all heard it down the pub, on the bus, in the shops -

> "EALTH AND SAFETY HAS GONE MAD MATE. Can't have a conker fight in school, can't put up hanging baskets in the park, can't blow your nose without some official idiot with a clipboard putting a stop to it because it is in breach of health and safety regulations."

Yes, we probably all have examples of "health and safety gone mad" but why is that? Is it complacency, ignorance, fear or plain old fashioned backside covering?

So let's cover each of these one by one using Personal Protective Equipment (PPE) as an example-

Complacency- We all know PPE is a last result but an essential part of keeping people safe. However, incorrectly used, issued or worn it's as good as a chocolate fire guard. How many times have you walked past road repairs and seen a tradesman cutting a paving slab with safety goggles on top of his head, how many times have you seen a construction site worker wearing his safety hat the wrong way round like some kind of fashion statement. These are classic examples of deep rooted complacency which has gone unchecked, unsupervised and unmanaged. When you see examples like this, you'd be correct in thinking that somewhere in the background there is a person responsible for health and safety that, for whatever reason is happy to leave things as they are. That person, through complacency, is allowing the tail to wag the dog. In other words, that person is allowing the employee to dictate how PPE should or shouldn't be worn.

Ignorance- Regulations and rules are often used in the same context. I have often been asked or told to do something because it's a health and safety regulation, when in fact it's a company rule interpreted from a regulation, sometimes correctly sometimes incorrectly.

I once went into a cafe. I stood by the counter and ordered a cup of coffee. Still standing at the counter, the young lady brought my coffee to me in a plastic cup. She placed the coffee on the counter and was about to put a plastic lid on the cup. Thinking environmentally and waste, I said-
"Don't bother with the lid, I'm not taking it out"
"No you must have a lid in case you spill it walking to your table" she said
"But I'm sitting right here, right next to the counter, no walking involved"
"Sorry its health and safety regulations"
Feeling a bit cheeky I said-
"What regulations say I must have a lid on my coffee cup?"
"It's all there in the regulations, you should read them" She said.
I left it at that.

You see, over the year's health and safety has been given a bad name and sometimes it has become a joke, not because of the regulations in place but the interpretation of those regulations. Regulations themselves are not complicated; it's when someone wades in without thought or reason that the problems start

Fear- I once surveyed a manufacturing company just before the Christmas shut down. After an initial meeting I asked to have a tour of the factory. It was a reasonable size factory with several large machines. Nearing the Christmas shut down, there was no production work going on. Instead employees were cleaning up but mainly painting machinery. As I walked round the one thing that stood out was everyone was wearing ear defenders, why? I thought. I paused, turned to the manager giving me the tour and asked the question-
"Why are people wearing ear defenders?"
He was quick to respond and the conversation went something like this-
"Under the Noise at Work Regulations all employees working in this area are required to wear ear defenders"
"Yes but why" I replied
"Because of the high levels of noise" he said
"But they are painting, there is no noise"
"Yes, but this is a noise zone area, we have signs to say wear ear defenders"
"Yes, but there is no noise, all the machines are shut off and they are painting, so why are they wearing ear defenders?"

"Well I will look into it but I'm sure ear defenders are required at all times"
"So why didn't you issue me with a pair and why aren't you wearing them?
"Good question, I see what you mean" he replied

I know this seems totally ridiculous but it's true. Here we had a manager who, for some reason, couldn't think outside the box. In his head, regulations required this because the signs said it was a noise zone area, regardless of whether there was noise or not employees were required to wear ear defenders.

Backside Covering- I think "Backside Covering" is the main reason for making health and safety look "bonkers" in the eyes of many.

How many times have you seen PPE being worn when there is no need to do so? My favourite is the MP or council leader conducting a TV interview.

There they are standing in front of the TV cameras in the middle of an open countryside field, fully kitted out, hard hat, hi-vis, safety boots the lot, explaining, where a new motorway is planned to run. There is no construction going on, no vehicles, just grass, trees and an open sky. Why I ask myself? I can only assume that somewhere some overeager safety person was mindful of potentially thousands of people watching the TV interview and was attempting to cover all eventualities in case an accident happened in front of the cameras. Someone could possibly be hit by a tractor, hence the hi-vis coat. Possibly be hit by a falling meteorite, hence the hard hat. Possibly hit in the eye by a passing bird, hence the safety glasses or maybe a camera would be dropped and fall on their toes hence, the safety boots.

This type of thing is not uncommon. I can remember being on holiday in the Peak District. It was a lovely day, blue sky, sun shining. I was standing by my car waiting for my wife who was in a small village shop buying some supplies. As I stood there a guy from the council came walking down the road, he was looking at road sign and making notes. As he passed me I said good morning and politely enquired as to what he was doing –

"Checking the road signs for wear and damage" he said

"You must be warm with all that PPE on" I said

"Health and safety" he replied "Health and safety"

This guy was wearing a hi-vis jacket, hard hat, safety footwear, safety glasses and ear plugs. His job was to walk along the pavement, look at the road signs and note any deficiencies. For what possible reason was he wearing all this gear. I can understand the hi-vis but surly the coat could have been replaced by a lightweight vest. I can understand the safety footwear as standard but why the hard hat? Was a sign liable to fall and hit him on the head? Why the safety glasses? Was he going to poke his eyes out with his pen? And why the ear plugs? Was he expecting a sign to crash to the ground making such a noise so as to damage his ear drums? No, this was a classic example of someone somewhere in an office covering their backside with little thought for the poor soul wearing all this unnecessary PPE in the hot summer sun.

When health and safety is taken to this extreme, and it is on so many occasions, it is little wonder that health and safety is said to be, by many,
"Gone mad "

Health and safety is often misused; being used as a reason or an excuse that an activity cannot take place or why something must be done a certain way. No Christmas lights in the works canteen in case of fire, running banned in the school playground, the list is endless. The fact is, these ill-considered, over the top decisions made in the name of health and safety, do in fact divert attention from the real risks to people at work. Real risks that lead not just to ill health, injury and suffering but also add to business overheads and affect profitability and diminish the hard work carried out by many to help protect people at work.

Chapter 17
Communicating The Safety Message

Communicating the safety message is no easy task, but crucial to creating a safe and healthy place to work. Your safety message will have the power to help prevent injuries and illness, so I am sure you would agree that it is something that needs to be taken seriously.

Like any other part of the business, health and safety deserves the time and effort required to ensure that the message is clear, engaging, positive and informative. Failure to communicate about health and safety makes it become a subject that employees think they don't need to be concerned about. Poor communication will have a negative effect on health and safety:

You may find this hard to believe (tongue in cheek) but not many people find health and safety interesting. You know the type, you're at a party and someone says-
> "What do you do for a living?"
> "I'm a health and safety manager"

And they politely change the subject. Could be worse though, you could say you're an estate agent.
It's much the same at work, if you let it stay that way. So it's important that you understand your audience, how to get them engaged and how to keep them engaged. Communication is a two way thing so you need to listen as well as talk. It can be a real pain at times, you know, the guy your afraid to walk

past because he or she always has a problem but, it's important to listen to their concerns no matter how small.

Knowledge is power as someone once said. Health and safety is a serious business, but coming across all serious all the time is only going to get you so far and you will become a bore and we have enough of those in health and safety. Try to communicate positively in a language that the particular target understands. It's no good quoting bits of the Health and Safety Act to someone who has no knowledge of the subject and has no need to know. So it is important to be aware of any barriers that may prevent or hinder your health and safety message. While you may be used to the safety jargon and legislation, bear in mind that most employees won't be. Employees will only be able to absorb so much, so make sure you prioritise your messages and even better, put a plan in place on what you are going to communicate.

I was carrying out a survey on a company and the health and safety manager tried to blind me and others around me by quoting section after section of the H&S Act and regulation after regulation. As I told him, people don't want to know all that, they just want to know how to work safely, it's like buying a TV licence, you know you have to have one but you don't need to know what Act requires you to have one.

Try to communicate the good things that have been done along with future goals and use "we" instead of "I". Make it real for them and give them examples and don't forget, a little bit of humour goes a long way.

Be very clear with your communication. If your message lacks clarity and is confusing, an employee may not actually hear what you had intended them to hear and your message will have been wasted. If expectations are not clearly defined, then you may have the opposite result to your message. Be sure to express clearly what result you expect. Employees who confide in you with their concerns deserve to be listened to and not just "heard". If you communicate a safety message without having listened to employees, then the communication is incomplete and will not be successful.

The following are a few examples on how to communicate the safety massage-

- Send a monthly newsletter via email – if your employees have an email address, this is a great way of popping into their inbox once a month to keep them up to date on what's happening in the world of health and safety. Keep it short, interesting and fun.

I loved compiling monthly newsletters and always received positive comments. If I ever missed a month or was late publishing I always got asked "Where's the Newsletter?"

- Put some health and safety notice boards, up in prominent positions. When I say health and safety, keep them to just that, don't let them be taken over by other information.

Put up the biggest notice-boards practicable, the bigger the better, and in the right places, on the shop floor, in the canteen, in the foyer, where visitors can see them. Fill them with information but, keep it, in the main, light hearted and interesting. Use posters, cartoons and photos.

Make some spelling mistakes in some of the information. When someone tells you that you have made a mistake, and they will, you will know they have read the information.

If you have nothing new to put on the board, change the information around and make sure people see you doing this. Give it a couple of minutes and a small crowd will gather to see what's new; nothing but they won't know that.

- Toolbox talks – these off the cuff, non-formal meetings can work really well in the workplace. Try and make it a routine talk, covering a different but relevant topic each week/month. Keep them short but again interesting.

- Share case studies or incident reports. It's important for employees to understand the reality of what happens when safety goes wrong. When you share information about real events and real happenings, employees are more likely to take notice.

Be careful on the graphics, I once had an employee faint when I posted a picture, obtained from the internet, of a guy who had nailed one of his testicles to a roof truss when using a nail gun.

- Take pictures of safe actions. While it might be tempting to highlight the unsafe actions, safe actions are important too and it's nice to promote the positive actions that employees are taking every day to stay safe. A picture is worth a thousand words. You could include these in your newsletter.

The most important thing is to remember the potential and the power of good communication. Don't underestimate this power. Safety is not just another part of your business; it's about showing you care for the people and showing them they are worth it. If you want employees to buy into health and safety, get good at communicating the safety message, it will pay dividends.

Chapter 18
In Conclusion

As I said before, I have read many health and safety books, some having hundreds of pages, at the end of which, I had a job to remember what I had read, long words, endless references and statistics, reams of irrelevant things to pack the book out and make it look good value for money and to show the reader how knowledgeable the author is. Perhaps I'm being a little hard but I think you know what I mean.

This book isn't hundreds of pages long, mainly because I have always been a straight thinker and talker, why use a hundred words when one will do? Why confuse the reader to prove your so called own in-depth knowledge of a subject.

I recently came across an old book, in my collection of books, which I purchased probably 30 years ago, on health and safety for beginners. I had a read through and was amused that after 30 years in the profession I still couldn't understand half of what was written. When I first read it, as a beginner, I must have been terrified. Hopefully this book hasn't been like that for you.

I promised from the start that this book would be a little different to the normal health and safety books out there. I promised it would be interesting non-jargonal; if there is such a word, and a little humorous. I hope it's been all of these things for you but most importantly, I hope you have learnt a little from my experiences and mistakes and can use this to your advantage.

Too many times I have met so called health and safety experts, who because they have a qualification belong to IOSH and have a brain for remembering the information most of us only need for exams, believe they really are experts. Too many times I have seen these people plodding along in their own little world believing, because they have a list of ISO's everything is safe and well on the shop floor, without having the need to go down on the shop floor and see for themselves. Too many times I have seen these people blag their way through the day and when the going gets tough, move on to the next poor unsuspecting company.

Hopefully this book has given you some food for thought about what it takes to be a successful health and safety manager. One that gets out of the office and on to the shop floor, one that talks to people, involves people and takes on new ideas. One that isn't afraid to get their hands dirty, one that isn't afraid to fight their corner, one that isn't too good to sit in the works canteen or shed, as it may be, and have a cup of tea and a chat with the lads or lasses. You will learn far more that way than you will from any book, no matter how many pages.

Be Safe and remember - Wear that cap with pride

Eric J Ward

Eric J Ward
Wardy Publications (2020)
wardypublications@gmail.com

Food for Thought
As a child I moaned because I had no shoes, then one day I met a boy with no feet (*Eric Ward* 1950 to 20??)

www.ingramcontent.com/pod-product-compliance
Lightning Source LLC
Chambersburg PA
CBHW071416210526
45465CB00001B/419